# Serving Up Some Funny Leftovers

Lisa DeMarco

Strategic Book Group
Durham, Connecticut

Strategic Book Group
P.O. Box 333
Durham CT 06422
www.StrategicBookClub.com

ISBN 978-1-60976-790-7

Printed in the United States of America

# Dedication

To all the FABULOUS people that have lived "One hell of a lifetime," thank you for allowing me to be part of your GRAND ADVENTURE. I take you with me always to remind me of the laughter.

A very special thanks also to Maggie Lassiter for giving me the encouragement I needed to finally publish my collection.

Since I finally managed to talk my way into getting a legal contract to professionally publish my first book, *Serving Up Some Funny*, I decided it was time to get started working on Part Two. Just think how proud my beloved father will be up in the heavens knowing that all the hard-earned money he spent on my college tuition really did not go to waste. I now not only have proof that I can do more than just write a "guest check" with my degree in Print Journalism that he paid for, but I actually have an AGENT!

I always knew *Serving Up Some Funny* would be successful, but I never realized how my little book of dirty jokes was going to affect my tiny lake community. When I first started working on the book nearly eight years ago, customers seemed excited to come into the restaurant where I worked to ask me if I had a new joke, which I always did. They would sit down for coffee or lunch, and we'd share our daily jokes. After a few years, though, mainly when the snowbirds returned each year, certain regulars started regularly asking me, "Whatever happened to that joke book?" (referring to the book formally known as *A Waitress's Collection of Jokes—Dirty Enough to Tell at the Breakfast Table*).

One day I finally took all the jokes I had already typed up (about fifty pages), and I paid to have photocopies made and bound. Then, while at work, I sold them out of the back of my Jeep—very quickly, I might add. I sold thirty copies in less than two days. Customers came in and asked about the book. I told them I had an "unedited edition." They wanted it. One older couple, who later became very dear friends, paid me double what I was charging ($5/cost), and then they came back the next day and bought another copy to send to friends up north. Not bad for someone who wasn't even really trying.

The project seemed to take on a life of its own, and many people were involved in creating it. Customers, co-workers, family members—everyone shared jokes with me, brought me in copies of jokes someone else had given them, or were simply forced to hear me tell one of my many "House Specialties." I sometimes told jokes several times a day because depending on how funny I thought a certain joke was determined how often I would repeat it. If I really liked it, I could tell that same joke all

5

day to every customer who I thought would enjoy it even if they weren't sitting in my station. Some jokes even managed to make it into my "Joke of the Week" or "Joke of the Month" category. Yet somehow, despite all my material, I published barely half the jokes I had collected. And now I'm stuck with an enormous pile of "leftovers."

So, for all those jokes that never got into *Serving Up Some Funny,* and to all those people who gave me jokes that didn't make it into that book, here is your chance to see your joke in print. Sorry it didn't make it last time but, as I always try to explain, I am a much better joke teller than I am a writer. If only my hands could type as fast as my mouth moves—I could surely kick out a book a month. Considering I do not type well, my computer skills are severely lacking, and I know nothing about the publishing industry, it is amazing that my writing career has come this far.

As always, please judge this book on its ability to entertain you through humor and laughter, and not necessarily with perfect grammar or punctuation. I am not sure which is actually the bigger limitation: my own editing skills or my lack of an editing budget. Nonetheless, thanks to the help of a select group of fine people whom I managed to convince to help me after much relentless pestering, I think it is looking pretty good. It is not meant to be an English textbook, after all. Enjoy it for what it is worth—a laugh.

At the risk of sounding "preachy," it's not that I think my book is great simply because I wrote it. On the contrary, I am so very inspired by the men and women who continue to create these hysterical works of art; I merely want to serve them up for others to enjoy. Again, I admire you all, my "originators" (the unknown authors of my collection). Some day we will all meet and together we will laugh.

Over the years I have made up a couple of really good one-liners of my own that I can truly say I own a claim to, and I have even considered (in fantasy) being a stand-up comedian because I can REALLY talk and I have tons of "stupid" things to talk about. Considering all the people I see on a daily basis, I wouldn't even need to tell actual jokes—I could simply repeat all the "stupid" things I saw and heard all day at work, at home, on the radio, on the TV, and on the Internet, not to mention those voices within my own head. Tons of funny stories. But like I have said before, my true calling is simply to collect and repeat funny jokes for others to enjoy. Especially because at this time my family needs me to hang on to my "service" job, and I might not have one if I start writing about "stupid" people instead of "silly" jokes.

Either way, if there was one thing I would preach to everyone I meet, it would be to make time to LAUGH. Laughter is great, and it makes you feel great. It MUST be a scientific fact: people who take the time to laugh and enjoy life—even if it means indulging in "silly" behavior—just feel better. It gives the body and brain the time to refresh itself from the day-to-day miseries that we all have. People who can laugh at a simple joke, whether it is spicy or cheesy or somewhat tasteless, realize that life doesn't have to be SO serious all the time.

With that, take a moment and savor it.

# Table of Contents

Classmate ........................................................................ 13
Big Lighter ...................................................................... 14
Can't Fix Stupid ............................................................. 15
Blind Bunny .................................................................... 17
I'm Broke ........................................................................ 18
Seeing Farts .................................................................... 19
Indian Knowledge .......................................................... 20
What Religion Is Your Bra? ........................................... 21
Honesty ........................................................................... 22
Son-in-Law ..................................................................... 23
Baseball in Heaven ........................................................ 24
In the Dark ..................................................................... 26
Fiftieth Wedding Anniversary ....................................... 28
Housework ...................................................................... 29
Cowboy and the Lesbian ............................................... 30
Ride a Cowboy ............................................................... 31
Shingles .......................................................................... 32
Birthday Wish ................................................................ 33
Men Don't Listen ........................................................... 34
Sick Leave ...................................................................... 35
Little Girl ....................................................................... 36
New C.E.O. ..................................................................... 37
What Went Wrong? ........................................................ 38
Heaven or Hell ............................................................... 39
Medical Exams ............................................................... 40
The Elderly ..................................................................... 42
Smart Comments ............................................................ 45
A Mother's Love ............................................................ 47

Divorced Barbie ....................................................... 48
Parking in a Snow Storm ...................................... 49
Twenty-Five Kids .................................................. 51
Billy Times Five .................................................... 52
Dream Girl ............................................................ 53
Twenty-Pound Baby Boy ...................................... 54
At the Vet .............................................................. 55
Poor Willie ............................................................ 56
Brain Surgery ........................................................ 57
Grocery Store Murder ........................................... 58
That's Bad .............................................................. 60
Handle It ................................................................ 62
Bubba ..................................................................... 63
New Orleans Crabs ................................................ 64
Gynecologist Assistant .......................................... 65
Good Golf Wife ..................................................... 66
Spaghetti ................................................................ 67
A New Bike ............................................................ 68
Men's Health Study ............................................... 69
Southern Choke ..................................................... 70
Herding .................................................................. 71
Two Woodpeckers ................................................. 73
Hypnosis ................................................................ 74
Italian Paramedics ................................................. 75
Getting a Dog ........................................................ 76
Vocabulary ............................................................ 77
Boys and Girls ....................................................... 78
Children ................................................................. 79
Not My Brother ..................................................... 81
Replacng Nursing Homes ..................................... 82
Digging Ditches ..................................................... 83
Living to Be Ninety .............................................. 84
Oh, Really ............................................................. 85
Interview ................................................................ 87
Rewind ................................................................... 89
Sniffer .................................................................... 91
Following Directions ............................................ 93
The Fire Engine ..................................................... 94

'Twas the Night of Thanksgiving ............................... 95
Cannibals .................................................................. 96
Thinking Back .......................................................... 97
The Parrot ................................................................ 98
I Promised ............................................................... 99
Banking .................................................................. 100
Neighborly Chat ..................................................... 102
Valuable Lesson ..................................................... 103
Preaching to the Bears ........................................... 105
Getting into Heaven ............................................... 107
Preacher's Wife ...................................................... 108
Nosey ..................................................................... 109
I'll Feed You ........................................................... 110
Blonde Officer ........................................................ 111
Sex of a Fly ............................................................ 112
Little Boy Choking ................................................. 113
Modern Technology ............................................... 114
Remedy .................................................................. 115
Because I'm Blonde? .............................................. 116
Pass Him ................................................................ 117
Message from Santa ............................................... 119
Goats ...................................................................... 120
The Baptist Cowgirl ............................................... 121
Woman Volunteer .................................................. 122
Marketing ............................................................... 123
Letters from Camp ................................................. 124
The Birds and the Bees .......................................... 126
BJ ........................................................................... 127

# Classmate

Have you ever been guilty of looking at others your own age and thinking, *I surely can't look that old?*

One day a lady was sitting in the waiting room for her first appointment with a new dentist. She noticed his DDS diploma, which stated his full name. Suddenly she remembered a tall, handsome, dark-haired boy with the same name who had been in her high school class some thirty-odd years ago. Could he be the same guy that she had a secret crush on way back then?

Upon seeing him, however, she quickly discarded any such thought. This balding, gray-haired man with a deeply lined face was too old to have been her classmate. After he examined her teeth, she asked him if he had attended her high school. "Yes. Yes, I did," he smiled, gleaming with pride.

"When did you graduate?" she asked.

He answered, "In 1975. Why do you ask?"

"You were in my class!" she exclaimed.

He looked at her a little closer, then that old, bald and wrinkled, fat-assed S.O.B. asked, "What did you teach?"

# Big Lighter

Olef and Sven were ice fishing in Michigan when Sven pulled out a cigar. Finding he had no matches, he asked Olef for a light. "Ya, shure, I think I haff a lighter," Olef replied, as he reached into his pocket and pulled out a lighter ten inches long.

"Yiminy Cricket," exclaimed Sven, taking the huge lighter in his hand. "Vere did yew git dat monster?"

"Vell," Olef replied, "I got it from my genie."

"You haff a genie?" Sven asked.

"Ya, shure. It's right here in my tackle box," said Olef.

"Could I see him?"

Olef opened his tackle box and sure enough out popped the genie. Addressing the genie, Sven said, "Hey dere, I'm a good friend of your master. Vill you grant me vun vish?"

"Yes, I will," said the genie.

So Sven asked the genie for a million bucks.

The genie disappeared back into the tackle box, leaving Sven sitting there waiting for his million bucks. Shortly the sky darkened and was filled with the sound of a million ducks flying directly overhead. Over the roar of the million ducks, Sven yelled to Olef, "Yumpin' yiminy, I asked for a million bucks, not a million ducks!"

Olef answers, "Ya, I forgot to tell yew dat da genie is hard of hearing. Do yew really tink I vished for a ten-inch Bic?"

# Can't Fix Stupid

Recently, while in a fast food restaurant, I saw on the menu that I could have an order of six, nine, or twelve chicken nuggets. I asked for a half dozen. "We don't have half dozens," said the teenaged girl working at the counter.

"You don't?" I replied.

"We only have six, nine, and twelve," she said.

"So I can't order half a dozen nuggets, but I can order six?"

"That's right," she answered with a smile.

I shook my head and ordered six nuggets.

A lady at work was seen putting a credit card into her floppy drive and pulling it out quickly. When I inquired what she was doing, she said, "I was shopping on the Internet, and they kept asking for my credit card number. So I was using the ATM thingy."

I was once in a car dealership when a large motor home was towed into the service department. The front of the vehicle was in dire need of repair and the whole thing generally looked like it had gone through a tornado. I asked the manager what had happened. He told me that the driver had set the cruise control and then went in the back to eat a sandwich.

My neighbor worked in the operations department in the central office of a large bank. Employees in the field called him when they had problems with their computers. One night he got a call from a woman in one of the branch banks. She had a question: "I've got smoke coming from the back of my terminal," she said. "Do you guys have a fire downtown?"

Police interrogated a suspect by placing a metal colander on his head and connecting it with wires to the photocopy machine. A piece of paper bearing the message "He is lying" was placed on the copier's glass, and the police pressed the copy button each time they thought he wasn't telling the truth. Believing the "lie detector" was working, the suspect confessed.

# Blind Bunny

One morning a blind bunny was hopping down the trail and tripped over a large snake. He fell right on his twitchy little nose. "Oh, please excuse me," the bunny said. "I didn't mean to trip over you, but I am blind and can't see."

"That's perfectly all right," replied the snake. "I'm sure it was my fault. I didn't mean to trip you, but I am blind too, and I didn't see you coming. By the way, what kind of animal are you?"

"Well, I really don't know," the bunny said. "I am blind, and I have never seen myself. Maybe you could examine me and find out."

So the snake felt the bunny all over, and said, "Well, you are soft and cuddly, and you have long ears, a little fluffy tail, and a small twitching nose. You must be a bunny rabbit."

The bunny said, "I can't thank you enough. But, by the way, what kind of animal are you?" he asked.

The snake replied that he didn't know either, so the bunny agreed to examine him, and when the bunny was finished the snake asked, "Well, what kind of animal am I?"

The bunny had felt the snake all over and he replied, "You are cold, slippery, and you have no balls. You must be a politician."

# I'm Broke

I answered a knock on the door yesterday, only to be confronted by a well-dressed young man carrying a vacuum cleaner. "Good morning," said the young man. "If I could take a couple of minutes of your time, I would like to demonstrate the very latest in high-powered vacuum cleaners."

"Go away!" I said. "I haven't got any money. I am broke!" I yelled as I proceeded to close the door.

Quick as a flash, the young man wedged his foot in the door and pushed it wide open. "Don't be too hasty," he said. "Not until you have at least seen my demonstration." And with that, he emptied a large bucket of horse manure onto my hallway carpet.

"If this vacuum cleaner does not remove every trace of this horse manure from your carpet, I will personally eat the remainder."

I stepped back and said, "Well, I hope you've got a friggin' good appetite, because they cut off my electricity this morning."

# Seeing a Fart

A little boy blows up a balloon and starts flicking it all around the house with his finger. His mother tells him to stop it because he is liable to break something, but the boy continues.

"Knock it off!" the mom screams. "You are going to break something!"

He stops, and eventually his mom leaves for a short trip to the shopping center. The boy starts up with the balloon again as soon as his mother leaves. He gives it one last flick and it lands in the toilet, where he leaves it. Mom comes in and while putting away the groceries she gets the urge, a diarrhea run. She can hardly make it to the toilet in time and splash, out it comes.

When she is finished, she looks down and can't believe what she is seeing. She's not sure what this big brown thing is in the toilet. She calls her doctor. The doctor is baffled as she describes the situation, but he assures her he'll be over shortly and examine everything.

When he arrives, Mom leads him to the bathroom and he gets down on his knees and takes a long hard look at the thing. Finally, he takes out his pen and sort of touches it to see what might happen. It pops. The balloon explodes and poop flies everywhere—on him, the walls, etc.

"Doctor! Doctor! Are you all right?" she asks.

He replies, "I have been in this business for over thirty years, and this is the first time I have ever actually seen a fart."

# Indian Knowledge

The Lone Ranger and Tonto go camping in the desert. After they get their tent set up, both men fall asleep. Some hours later, Tonto wakes. He says, "Kemo Sabe, look toward the sky. What do you see?"

The Lone Ranger replies, "I see millions of stars."

"What does that tell you?" asks Tonto.

The Lone Ranger ponders for a minute and says, "Astronomically speaking, it tells me there are millions of galaxies. Time-wise, it appears approximately a quarter past three in the morning. Theologically, the Lord is all-powerful, and we are small and insignificant. Meteorologically, it seems we will have a beautiful day tomorrow. What does it tell you, Tonto?"

"That you are dumber than buffalo shit. Someone stole the tent."

# What Religion Is Your Bra?

A man walked into the ladies' department of a local clothing store. He shyly approached the woman behind the counter and said, "I would like to buy a bra for my wife."

"What type of bra?" asked the clerk.

"Type?" the man inquired. "There is more than one type?"

"Look around," the saleslady said, and she indicated a sea of bras in every shape, size, color, and material imaginable.

"Actually, even with all this variety, there really are only four types to choose from."

Relieved, the man asked about the types. The saleslady replied, "There are the Catholic bras, the Salvation Army bras, the Presbyterian bras, and the Baptist bras. Which one would you prefer?"

Now totally confused, the man asked about the differences between them. The saleslady responded, "It is all really quite simple. The Catholic bra supports the masses. The Salvation Army bra lifts the fallen. The Presbyterian bra keeps them staunch and upright, and the Baptist bra makes mountains out of mole hills."

Recently, Germany has also added their own type of bra, the "Holtzemfromfloppen."

# Honesty

A married couple were sitting watching TV. The husband turned to his wife and said, "Honey, tell me something that will make me happy and sad at the same time."

She turned to him and said, "You have the biggest dick of all your friends."

# Son-in-Law

As a woman passed her daughter's closed bedroom door, she heard a strange buzzing noise coming from within. Opening the door, she observed her daughter with a vibrator. Shocked, she asked, "What in the world are you doing?"

The daughter replied, "Mom, I'm thirty-five years old, unmarried, and still living with my parents. This thing is about as close as I'll ever get to a husband. Please, go away and leave me alone."

The next day, the girl's father heard the same buzzing coming from behind the closed bedroom door. Upon entering the room, he observed his daughter passionately enjoying her vibrator. To his query as to what she was doing, the daughter said, "Dad, I am thirty-five, unmarried, and still living with my parents. This thing is about as close as I'll ever get to a husband. Please, go away and leave me alone."

A couple of days later, the wife came home from a shopping trip, placed the groceries on the kitchen counter, and heard that buzzing noise coming from—of all places—the living room. She entered that area and observed her husband sitting on the couch, drinking a cold beer, and staring at the television set. The vibrator was next to him on the couch, buzzing like crazy.

The wife asked, "What the hell are you doing?"

"I'm watching football with my son-in-law," the husband replied.

# Baseball in Heaven

Two ninety-year-old men, Sam and Moe, have been friends their whole lives. Sam is dying, and Moe comes to visit him every day. "Sam," says Moe, "you know how we both loved baseball all our lives, and how we played together for so many years. Sam, you have to do me one favor. When you get to Heaven—and I know you will go to Heaven—somehow you've got to let me know if there's baseball up there."

Sam looks at Moe from his deathbed and says, "Moe, you've been my best friend for so many years. This favor, if it is at all possible, I'll do for you."

Shortly thereafter, Sam passes on.

At midnight a couple of nights later Moe is sound asleep when he is awakened by a blinding light and a voice calling out to him. "Moe. Moe," it says.

"Who is it?" Moe asks, sitting up suddenly. "Who is it?"

"Moe, it's me—Sam."

"Come on. You're not Sam. Sam just died."

"I'm telling you," insists the voice. "It is me, SAM."

"Sam? Is that you? Where are you?"

"I'm in Heaven," says Sam, "and I've got to tell you something. I've got really good news and a little bad news."

"So tell me the good news first," says Moe.

"The good news is that there is baseball in Heaven. Better yet, all our old buddies who've gone before us are here. Better yet, we're all young men again. Better yet, it's always springtime and it never rains or snows. And best of all, we can play baseball all we want, and we never get tired," he says.

"Really?" says Moe. "That is fantastic, wonderful beyond my wildest dreams. But what's the bad news?"

"You're pitching next Tuesday."

# In the Dark

A woman takes her lover home during the day, while her husband is at work. Her nine-year-old son comes home unexpectedly. He sees them in bed and hides in the bedroom closet to watch. The woman's husband also comes home early. She puts her lover in the closet, not realizing that her son is already in there.

The little boy says, "Dark in here."

The man says, "Yes, it is."

Boy says, "I have a baseball."

Man says, "That's nice."

Boy says, "Want to buy it?"

Man says, "No, thanks."

Boy says, "My dad's outside."

Man says, "Okay, how much?"

Boy says, "$250."

A few weeks later, the boy and the lover again find themselves hiding in the closet together. The boy says, "Dark in here."

Man says, "Yes, it is."

Boy says, "I have a baseball glove."

The lover, remembering the last time, asks the boy, "How much?"

Boy says, "$750."

Man says, "Sold."

A few days later, the father says to the boy, "Grab your glove, let's go outside and have a game of catch."

The boy says, "I can't. I sold my baseball and my baseball glove."

The father asks, "How much did you get for them?"

Boy answers, "$1,000."

The father says, "That's terrible to overcharge your friends like that. That is way more than those things cost. I'm going to take you to church and make you confess."

They go to church and the father makes the little boy sit in the confessional and he closes the door. The boy says, "Dark in here."

The priest says, "Don't start that crap again—you're in my closet now."

# Fiftieth Anniversary

A man and his wife were celebrating fifty years together. Their three children, all very successful, agreed to a Sunday dinner in their honor. "Happy Anniversary, Mom and Dad," gushed son number one. "Sorry I'm running late. I had an emergency at the hospital— you know how it is. Sorry I didn't have the time to get a gift."

"Not to worry," said the father. "The important thing is that we're all together today."

Son number two arrived. "You and Mom look great, Dad. I just flew in from Los Angeles between depositions. I didn't have time to shop for you. Sorry," he said.

"It's nothing," said the father. "We're glad you were able to come."

Just then the daughter arrived. "Hello and Happy Anniversary. I'm sorry, but my boss is sending me out of town, and I was really busy packing, so I didn't have time to get you anything."

Again the father said, "It's okay. We're just happy to have you all together."

After they finished dessert, the father said, "May I have your attention? There is something your mother and I have wanted to tell you all for a long time. You see, we started out our life together very poor. Despite this, we always gave you three everything you ever needed growing up, and we managed to send each of you to college. Throughout the years your mother and I worked hard and stayed busy in order to ensure our lavish lifestyle, but we just never found the time to get married."

The three adult children gasped and said in unison, "You mean we're bastards?"

"Yep," the father said. "And cheap ones, too."

# Housework

Housework was a woman's job in Jenny's marriage, but one evening she arrived home from work to find the children bathed, one load of laundry in the washing machine, and another in the dryer. Dinner was on the stove, and the table was set. She was astonished.

It turned out that Jenny's husband Chuck had read an article that said, "Wives who work full-time and have to do all the housework are too tired for sex."

That night went well and the next day she told her office friends all about it. "We had a great dinner. He even cleaned up. He helped the kids do their homework, folded all the laundry, and put it away. I really enjoyed the evening."

"And what about afterwards?" her friends asked.

"Oh, that—Chuck was way too tired."

# Cowboy and the Lesbian

An old cowboy sat down at the bar and ordered a drink. As he sat sipping his drink, a young woman sat down next to him. She turned to him and asked, "Are you a real cowboy?"

He replied, "Well, I've spent my whole life breaking colts, working cows, going to rodeos, fixing fences, pulling calves, bailing hay, doctoring animals, cleaning barns, fixing flats, working on tractors, and feeding my dog, so I guess I am a REAL cowboy."

She said, "I'm a lesbian. I spend my whole day thinking about woman. As soon as I get up in the morning, I think about women. When I shower, I think about women. When I watch TV, I think about women. I even think about women when I eat. It seems that everything makes me think of women."

The two sat in silence. A little while later, a man sat down on the other side of the old cowboy and asked, "Are you a real cowboy?"

He replied, "I always thought I was, but I just found out I'm a lesbian."

# Ride a Cowboy

Prior to her trip to Texas, Buffy (a northerner) confided to her co-workers that she had three goals on her trip to the Lone Star state:

1. She wanted to taste some real Texas bar-b-que.
2. She wanted to take in a bona fide rodeo.
3. She wanted to have sex with a real cowboy.

Upon her return, the girls were curious as to how she fared. "Let me tell you," she said. "They have a tree down there called mesquite, and they slow cook brisket over that mesquite, and it's ooooh so good. The taste is unbelievable. And I went to a rodeo. Talk about athletic! Those guys wrestle full-grown bulls. They ride horses at full gallop, then jump off the horse and grab the bull by the horns and throw him on the ground. It is just incredible."

Then they asked, "Well, tell us—did you have sex with a real cowboy?"

"Are you kidding? When I saw the outline of the condom they carried in the back pocket of their jeans, I changed my mind." (It was a Skoal chewing tobacco container.)

# Shingles

Bubba walked into the doctor's office, and the receptionist asked him what he had. Bubba said, "Shingles."

So she wrote down his name, address, and medical insurance number, and told him to have a seat. Fifteen minutes later, a nurse's aide came out and asked Bubba what he had. Bubba said, "Shingles."

So she wrote down his height, weight, and a complete medical history and told him to wait in the examining room. A half-hour later, a nurse came in and asked Bubba what he had. Bubba again said, "Shingles."

So the nurse gave Bubba a blood test, a blood pressure test, and an electrocardiogram, and told Bubba to take off all his clothes and wait for the doctor.

An hour later, the doctor finally came into the examining room and asked Bubba, "What do you have?"

Bubba replied, "Shingles."

The doctor asked, "Where?"

Bubba said, "Outside on the truck. Where do you want them?"

# Birthday Wish

A man was sitting on the edge of his bed, observing his wife turning front and back, looking at herself in the mirror. Since her birthday was not far off, he asked what she would like for her birthday.

"I'd like to be six again," she replied, still looking in the mirror.

On the morning of her birthday, her husband rose early, made her a nice big bowl of fruity cereal, and then took her to a theme park. What a day! He put her on every ride in the park: Death Slide, the Wall of Fear, the Screaming Monster Roller Coaster—everything there was. When they staggered out of the amusement park five hours later, her head was reeling and her stomach felt upside down.

The husband then took her to a fast-food restaurant where he ordered her a kiddie meal with extra fries and a chocolate shake. Then it was off to a movie, with popcorn, soda pop, and her favorite candies. What a fabulous adventure! Finally she wobbled home with her husband and collapsed into bed, exhausted.

He leaned over his wife with a big smile and lovingly asked, "Well, dear, what was it like being six again?"

Her eyes slowly opened and her expression suddenly changed. "I meant my dress size, dumb ass!"

# Men Don't Listen

While visiting a hospital, a gentleman made several attempts to get into the men's restroom but it was always occupied. A nurse noticed his predicament. "Sir," she said, "you may use the ladies' room if you promise not to touch any of the buttons on the wall."

He did what he needed to, and as he sat there he noticed the buttons he had promised not to touch. Each button was identified by letters: WW, WA, PP, and a red one labeled ATR. Who would know if he were to touch them? He couldn't resist. He pushed the WW button and warm water was sprayed gently upon his bottom. *What a nice feeling*, he thought. *Men's restrooms don't have nice things like this.*

Anticipating greater pleasure, he pushed the WA button. Warm air replaced the warm water, gently drying his underside. When this stopped, he pushed the PP button. A large powder puff caressed his bottom, adding a fragile scent of spring flowers to this unbelievable pleasure. The ladies' restroom was more than a restroom: it was a tender loving pleasure retreat.

When the powder puff completed its task, he couldn't wait to push the ATR button, which he knew would bring supreme ecstasy. Next thing he knew, he opened his eyes to find himself in a hospital bed, and the nurse was staring down at him. "What happened?" he exclaimed. "The last thing I remember was pushing the ATR button."

"The ATR button is the Automatic Tampon Remover. Your penis is under your pillow," she said.

# Sick Leave

I urgently needed a few days off work, but I knew the boss would not allow me to take any sick time. I thought that maybe if I acted crazy, he would tell me to take some leave. So I hung upside down from the ceiling and made funny noises. My co-worker (a blonde) asked me what I was doing. I told her that I was pretending to be a light bulb so that the boss would think I was crazy and give me a few days off.

A few minutes later the boss came into the office and asked, "What are you doing?"

I told him that I was a light bulb. He said, "You are clearly stressed out. Go home and recuperate for a couple of days."

I jumped down and walked out of the office. When my co-worker followed me, the boss said to her, "And where do you think you're going?"

She answered, "I'm going home, too—I can't work in the dark."

# Little Girl

A stranger was seated next to a little girl on an airplane. When the stranger turned to her and said, "Let's talk. I've heard that flights go quicker if you strike up a conversation with your fellow passengers."

The little girl, who had just opened her book, closed it slowly and said to the stranger, "What would you like to talk about?"

"Oh, I don't know," he said. "How about nuclear power?"

"Okay," she said. "That could be an interesting topic. But let me ask you a question first. A horse, a cow, and a deer all eat the same stuff: grass. Yet the deer excretes little pellets, while a cow turns out a flat patty, and a horse produces clumps of dry grass. Why do you suppose that is?"

The stranger, visibly surprised by the little girl's intelligence, thought about it and said, "Hmmm, I have no idea."

To which the little girl replied, "Do you really feel qualified to discuss nuclear power when you don't even know shit?"

# New C.E.O.

A large company, feeling it was time for a real shakeup, hired a new C.E.O. The new boss was determined to rid the company of all slackers. On a tour of the facilities, the C.E.O. noticed a guy leaning on a wall. The room was full of workers and he wanted to let them all know that he meant business. He walked up to the guy leaning against the wall and asked, "How much do you make a week?"

A little surprised, the young man looked at him and said, "I make $400 a week. Why?"

The C.E.O. then handed the guy $1,600 in cash and screamed, "Here's four weeks' pay. Now GET OUT and don't come back!"

Feeling pretty good about himself, the C.E.O. looked around the room and asked, "Does anyone want to tell me what that goofball did around here?"

From across the room came a voice, "He was delivering pizza."

# What Went Wrong?

An Indian chief was asked by a white U.S. government official, "You have observed the white man for over ninety years. You've seen his wars and his advanced technology. You've seen his progress and the damage he has done."

The chief nodded in agreement.

The official continued, "Considering all these events, in your opinion where did the white man go wrong?"

The chief stared at the government official for over a minute then calmly replied, "When the white man find land, Indians running it, no taxes. No debt, plenty of buffalo, plenty of beaver, clean water. Women did all the work. Medicine man was free. Indian men spent all day fishing and hunting, all night having sex." Then the chief leaned back and smiled, "Only white man dumb enough to think he could improve system like that."

# Heaven or Hell

An old lady dies and goes to Heaven. She is chatting with Saint Peter at the pearly gates when all of a sudden she hears the most awful, blood-curdling scream. "Don't worry about that," Saint Peter assures her. "It is only someone having the holes put into their shoulder blades for their wings."

The old lady, looking a little uncomfortable, carries on with the conversation. Ten minutes later there are more blood-curdling screams. "Oh my God!" cries the woman. "Now what is happening?"

"Not to worry," Saint Peter replies. "Someone's just having his head drilled to fit his halo."

"I can't do this!" she protests. "I'm going to hell!"

"You can't go there!" Saint Peter objects. "You'll be raped and taken advantage of."

"Maybe so," answers the old lady, "but I've already got the holes for that."

# Medical Exams

A man comes into the ER and yells, "My wife's going to have our baby in the cab!"

The doctor grabs his stuff, rushes out to the cab, lifts the lady's dress, and begins to take off her underwear. Suddenly he notices that there are several cabs in the driveway, and that he is in the wrong one." (By Dr. Mark McDonald)

At the beginning of his shift, a doctor placed a stethoscope on an elderly and slightly deaf female patient's anterior chest wall. "Big breaths," he instructed.

"Yes, they used to be," the lady said. (By Dr. Richard Byrnes)

One day a doctor had to be the bearer of bad news. He had to tell a woman that her husband had died of a massive myocardial infarction. Not more than five minutes later, he heard her reporting to the rest of the family that he had died of a "massive internal fart." (By Dr. Susan Steinberg)

During a patient's two-week follow-up appointment with his cardiologist, he informed his doctor that he was having trouble with one of the medications. "Which one?" the doctor asked.

"The patch. The nurse told me to put on a new one every six hours and now I am running out of places to put them."

Quickly, the doctor had him undress and, sure enough, he discovered what he hoped he wouldn't see. Yes, the man had over fifty patches on his body.

Now the usage instructions include a step to remove old patches before applying a new one. (By Dr. Rebecca St. Clair)

While acquainting himself with a new elderly patient, a doctor asked, "How long have you been bedridden?"

With a look of complete confusion, she answered, "Why, not for at least twenty years, when my husband was still alive." (By Dr. Steven Swanson)

A doctor was performing rounds at a hospital one morning and while checking up on a woman, he asked, "So how's your breakfast this morning?"

"It's very good, except for the Kentucky Jelly. I can't seem to get used to the taste," the patient replied.

He then asked to see the jelly. The woman produced a foil packet labeled, "KY Jelly." (By Leonard Kransdorf)

A young doctor doing his residency in OB was quite embarrassed when performing female pelvic exams. In his embarrassment he had unconsciously formed a habit of whistling softly. One day, the middle-aged lady whom he was examining suddenly burst out laughing. He looked up from his work sheepishly and said, "I'm sorry, was I tickling you?"

She replied, "No, doc, but the song you were whistling was 'I Wish I Were an Oscar Meyer Wiener.'" (Doctor unknown)

# The Elderly

An elderly gentleman had serious hearing problems for a number of years. He went to the doctor, and the doctor was able to have him fitted for a set of hearing aids that would allow him to hear 100%.

The elderly man went back in a month to the doctor and the doctor said, "Your hearing is perfect. Your family must be really pleased that you can hear again."

The gentleman replied, "Oh, I haven't told my family yet. I just sit around and listen to their conversations. I've changed my will three times already."

An elderly couple had dinner at another couple's house. After eating, the wives left the table and went into the kitchen. The two gentlemen were talking and one said, "Last night we went out to a new restaurant, and it was really great. I would recommend it very highly."

The other man asked, "What is the name of the restaurant?"

The first man thought and thought and finally said, "What is the name of that flower you give someone you love? You know, the one that's red and has thorns."

"Do you mean a rose?"

"Yes, that's the one," replied the man. He then turned toward the kitchen and yelled, "Rose, what's the name of that restaurant we went to last night?"

Hospital regulations require a wheelchair for patients being discharged. However, while working as a student nurse I found one elderly gentleman—already dressed and sitting on his bed with a suitcase at his feet—who insisted he didn't need my help to leave the hospital. After a chat about rules being rules, he reluctantly let me wheel him into the elevator. On the way down I asked him if his wife was meeting him.

"I don't know," he said. "She's still upstairs in the bathroom changing out of her hospital gown."

A couple in their nineties are both having problems remembering things. During a check-up, the doctor tells them that they are physically fit, but they might want to start writing things down to help them remember.

Later that night while watching TV, the old man gets up from his chair. "Want anything while I'm in the kitchen?" he asked his wife.

"Will you get me a bowl of ice cream?"

"Sure," he replied.

"Don't you think you should write it down so you can remember?" she asked.

"No, I can remember it."

"Well, I'd like some strawberries on top, too. Maybe you should write it down, so not to forget."

He yelled, "I can remember that! A bowl of ice cream with strawberries."

"I'd like some whipped cream, also, please. I'm certain you are going to forget. Write it down," she insisted.

Irritated, he said, "I don't need to write it down. I can remember it: a bowl of ice cream with strawberries and whipped cream. I got it, for goodness sake!"

Then he toddled into the kitchen. After about twenty minutes, the old man returned from the kitchen and handed his wife a plate of bacon and eggs. She stared at the plate for a moment. "Where's my toast?" she asked.

A senior citizen said to his eighty-year-old buddy, "So I hear you're getting married?"

"Yep."

"Do I know her?"

"Nope."

"This woman—is she good looking?"

"Not really."

"Is she a good cook?"

"Naw, she can't cook at all."

"Does she have a lot of money?"

"Nope. Poor as a church mouse."

"Well, then, is she good in bed?"

"I don't know."

"Why in the world do you want to marry her, then?"

"Because she can still drive."

Three old guys are out walking. First man says, "Windy, isn't it?"

Second man says, "No, it's Thursday."

Third man says, "So am I. Let's go get a beer."

A man is telling his neighbor, "I just bought a new hearing aid. It cost me four thousand dollars, but it's state of the art. It's perfect."

"Really?" the neighbor said. "What kind is it?"

"Twelve-thirty," he answered.

An eighty-two-year-old man went to the doctor to get a physical. A few days later, the doctor saw the same man walking down the street with a gorgeous young woman on his arm. A couple of days later, the doctor saw the man again with the same young woman. Finally, on the third day that the doctor saw the older man, he stopped him and said, "You're really doing great, aren't you?"

The older man replied that he was just doing what the doctor ordered: "Get a hot momma and be cheerful."

The doctor replied, "I didn't say that—I said you've got a heart murmur, be careful."

A little old man shuffled slowly into an ice cream parlor and pulled himself painfully up onto a stool. After catching his breath, he ordered a banana split. The waitress asked kindly, "Crushed nuts?"

"No," he replied. "Arthritis."

# Smart Comments

It was mealtime during an airplane flight. "Would you like some dinner?" asked the flight attendant to a gentleman seated in the front row.

"What are my choices?" he asked.

"Yes or no," she answered.

A flight attendant was stationed at the departure gate to check tickets. As a man approached, she extended her hand for his ticket. He opened his trench coat and flashed her. Without missing a beat, she said, "Sir, I need to see your ticket, not your stub."

The cop got out of his car and the kid who was stopped for speeding rolled down his window. "I've been waiting for you all day," the officer said.

The kid replied, "Yeah, well, I got here as fast as I could."

When the cop finally stopped laughing, he sent the young man on his way with a warning.

A college teacher reminds her class of tomorrow's final exam. "Now class, I won't tolerate any excuses for not being here tomorrow. I might consider a nuclear attack or a serious personal injury, illness, or a death in your immediate family, but that's it. No other excuses whatsoever."

A sassy student in the back of the room raises his hand and asks, "What would you say if tomorrow I said I was suffering from complete and utter sexual exhaustion?"

The entire class is reduced to laughter and snickering. When silence is restored, the teacher smiles knowingly at the student, shakes her head and sweetly says, "Well, I guess you'll have to write the exam with your other hand."

# A Mother's Love

A little boy asks his mother, "Mommy, how come I'm black and you're white?"

His mother bends down and looks her young son right in the eyes and says, "Don't even go there. From what I can remember about that night, you're lucky you don't bark."

# Divorced Barbie

One day a father gets out of work and on his way home he suddenly remembers that it's his daughter's birthday. He pulls over to a toy store and asks the saleswoman, "How much for the Barbies in the display window?"

The saleslady answers, "Which one do you mean, sir? We have Work-Out Barbie for $19.95, Shopping Barbie for $19.95, Beach Barbie for $19.95, Disco Barbie for $19.95, Ballerina Barbie for $19.95, and Divorced Barbie for $265.95."

The amazed father asks, "It's what? Why is the Divorced Barbie $265.95 and all the others are only $19.95?"

The annoyed salesclerk rolls her eyes, sighs, and answers, "Sir, Divorced Barbie comes with Ken's car, Ken's house, Ken's boat, Ken's furniture, Ken's computer, one of Ken's friends, and a key chain made from Ken's balls."

# Parking in a Snow Storm

The dumbest woman on the planet lived in upstate New York. She and her husband were home one afternoon. He was sitting in his chair in the living room reading the daily newspaper, just as he did every day, while she was tending to things in the kitchen. Over the radio an emergency announcement interrupted the song that was playing. It stated that there was going to be a very heavy snowstorm later that evening. To prepare for the morning, it requested all residents in the area to park their vehicles on the right side of the street so that the snowplows could easily get through. The woman heard the weather warning and scrambled around looking for her keys to quickly move her car. Her husband never even looked up from his paper. He just continued reading as if nothing had happened.

About a week later, a similar announcement came on the radio. This time, however, the announcer requested that all residents park their cars on the left side of the roadways in order to keep the path clear for the snowplows. Again, while her husband sat totally oblivious to the warning, his wife ran around the house like a chicken without her head, desperately trying to immediately move her car as instructed.

A few day later, a third broadcast came over the radio. The disc jockey announced that the National Weather Authority was issuing a "Severe Weather Warning" for the area. He stated that it was expected to be one of the worst snowstorms on record. He went on to predict that by daylight they were expected to have a couple of feet of fresh snow along with extreme winds and temperatures below freezing. He continued, "Authorities suggest that all residents kindly park their cars on the—"

But before the wife could hear which side of the road she was supposed to park on, the radio station went fuzzy and lost transmission. Panicked, she ran into the living room where her husband was quietly sitting in his chair. She appeared beyond confused. "I don't know where to park the car. He didn't tell me where to park the car!" she cried.

The husband calmly responded, "How about you just leave it in the garage this time?"

# Twenty-Five Kids

A lady gets married, and with her husband she has eight children. Soon after their last child is born, he dies. The woman re-marries, and with her second husband she has seven more children. Not long after their last child was born, the man dies. The woman marries a third time, and with this husband she has ten additional children. Now with twenty-five children, the woman again becomes a widow. Soon after, she passes away herself.

At her funeral service, two of her oldest and dearest girlfriends are talking. The one old lady says to the other, "At least now they will be together."

"Who will be together?" the other lady asks, a little confused.

"Her legs," the woman replies.

# Billy Times Five

Two young moms are at the local park, watching their children play on the playground. The one mom notices that the other woman has five sons, all named Billy. Amazed, the lady strikes up a conversation and asks, "Doesn't it get really confusing with all your boys having the same name?"

"No," she replies. "It actually makes it quite easy. When I want one of them to behave, I just yell 'Billy!' and they all hear me. And if I want them for supper, I just yell 'Billy!' and they all come running."

Intrigued, the woman asks, "But what do you do when you really only want one of the boys' attention?"

"Oh, that's easy," she says. "I just call him by his last name."

# Dream Girl

A very homely-looking man comes into the bar. He is UGLY, but he has the biggest shit-eatin' grin on his face. The barmaid asks him as he approaches the bar, "What the hell are you so happy about?"

The man smiles and says, "I just had the best sex I have ever had. I had sex in every position I could think of, and I feel like a lucky man."

"Good for you," the barmaid says. "Where did you meet her?"

"It was the strangest thing," he answers. "It was like a dream. I was walking alongside the railroad tracks and there she was. So I brought her home with me, and we had FABULOUS sex."

"Wow, that sounds great," she says, a little surprised considering how unattractive the man appears to be. "Was she pretty?" she asks.

The man answers, "I don't know—I haven't found the head yet."

# Twenty-Pound Baby Boy

A big country boy is hanging out at the local tavern which he frequents. He is playing pool and drinking beers when his cell phone rings. He happily announces to the entire bar that his wife just went into labor with their first child. He is thrilled. He tosses his cue onto the pool table, chugs down the rest of his open beer, and shouts, "Wish me luck!" as he exits the bar.

The next day the young man returns to brag about his first-born son. He boasts about his weighing in at a whopping twenty pounds. The entire bar is amazed by the child's birth weight. Even the bartender comments on how he feels for the little missus after giving birth to such a large baby. Proud as can be, the young man continues to tell everyone in the bar about his good fortune and the people continue buying him rounds of drinks to help him celebrate.

About a week later, the man returns. The bartender immediately strikes up a conversation with him about his son. "That boy of yours must be growing like a weed already. What's he weigh now?" he asks.

"Eighteen pounds," the man replies.

"Eighteen? Now that doesn't seem right—I thought you said he weighed twenty pounds at birth?"

"He did," the proud father says. "But we had him circumcised."

# At the Vet

Three dogs are caged in a waiting room at the local veterinarian's office. There is a Poodle, a Chihuahua, and a Great Dane. The Poodle asks the Chihuahua what he is there for. The Chihuahua replies that his owner is tired of hearing him yap. So he is there to have his vocal cords removed.

The Poodle says, "That sucks, but I guess it is better than being put down."

The Chihuahua agrees.

Then the Chihuahua asks the Poodle what he is there for. The Poodle tells him that his owner is sick and tired of him leaping around the house all the time, so he is there to have the tendons removed from his legs so that he could no longer jump around.

"Wow, that sucks," the Chihuahua says. "But I guess it is better than being put down."

The Poodle agrees.

Suddenly, the Poodle and the Chihuahua look at the Great Dane. "What are you in for?" the Poodle asks.

The Great Dane responds, "Well, the other day while my owner was bent over in the bathroom drying herself off after her shower, I mounted her."

The other two dogs gasped in shock. "So she brought you in to have you put down?" the Poodle asks sadly.

"No," the Dane answers, "To have my nails clipped."

# Poor Willie

Willie was an old cowboy who had lived a good life. He enjoyed his youth. He was successful as an adult, and he was now rather content relaxing through his retirement years. He had a good woman. He had a beautiful home, and he still enjoyed just sitting on his property simply looking at the great outdoors.

One day a young man who recently purchased the property next to Willie's stopped by to introduce himself. Willie was sitting on his porch swing, just looking out over his field of dandelions, when the young man approached. The young man had heard of Willie and knew of his standing in the rodeo. He considered it quite a privilege just to meet the famous old cowboy, and now he got to live right next door. Excited by the possibility of learning some great insight, the young man asked Willie, "Is there anything that you wish could have been different?"

Willie, without missing a beat, answered, "I just wish I didn't outlive my dick."

# Brain Surgery

In the hospital waiting room, the relatives of a gravely ill man gathered. Finally, the doctor came in, looking tired and somber. "I'm afraid I'm the bearer of bad news," he said as he surveyed the worried faces. "The only hope left for your loved one is a brain transplant. It's an experimental procedure, very risky, but it is the only hope. Insurance will cover the procedure, but you will have to pay for the brain yourselves."

The family members sat silent as they absorbed the news. After a length of time, someone asked, "Well, how much does a brain cost?"

The doctor quickly responded, "$5,000 for a male brain, and $200 for a female brain."

The moment turned awkward. The men in the room tried not to smile, avoiding eye contact with the women, but some actually smirked. A man unable to control his curiosity blurted out the question everyone wanted to ask, "Why does a male brain cost so much more?"

The doctor smiled and explained, "It's just standard pricing procedure. We have to mark down the price of the female brains because they've actually been used."

# Grocery Store Murder

Tired of constantly being broke and stuck in an unhappy marriage, a young husband decided to solve both problems by taking out a large insurance policy on his wife with himself as the beneficiary. Then he arranged to have her killed.

A "friend of a friend" put him in touch with a nefarious underworld figure who went by the name of "Artie."

Artie explained to the husband that his going price for snuffing out a spouse was $5,000. The husband said he was willing to pay that amount, but that he wouldn't have any cash on hand until he collected his wife's insurance money.

Artie insisted on being paid at least something up front, so the man opened his wallet, displaying the single dollar bill that rested inside. Artie sighed, rolled his eyes, and reluctantly agreed to accept the dollar as a down payment for the dirty deed.

A few days later, Artie followed the man's wife to the local grocery store. He surprised her in the produce department and proceeded to strangle her with his gloved hands. As the poor, unsuspecting woman drew her last breath and slumped to the floor, the manager of the produce department stumbled onto the murder scene. Unwilling to leave any living witnesses behind, Artie had no choice but to strangle the store employee as well.

However, unknown to Artie, the entire proceedings were captured by hidden security cameras and observed by the store's security guard, who immediately called the police. Artie was caught and arrested before he could even leave the building.

Under intense questioning at the police station, Artie revealed the whole sordid plan, including his unusual financial arrangements with the hopeless husband who was also quickly arrested.

The next day in the newspaper the headline declared, "Artie Chokes 2 for $1.00."

# That's Bad

Two guys were discussing popular family trends on sex, marriage, and values. Bob said, "I didn't sleep with my wife before we got married. Did you?"

Mark replied, "I'm not sure—what was her maiden name?"

A little boy went to his father and asked, "Dad, where did my intelligence come from?"

The father replied, "Well, son, you must have gotten it from your mother because I still have mine."

"Mr. Clark, I have reviewed this case very carefully," the divorce court judge said, "and I've decided to give your wife $775 a week."

"That's very fair, your honor," the husband said. "And every now and then, I'll try to send her a few bucks myself."

A doctor, examining a woman who had been rushed to the Emergency Room, took the husband aside and said, "I don't like the looks of your wife at all."

"Me neither, doc," the husband said, "but she's a great cook and really good with the kids."

An old man goes to a wizard to ask him if he can remove a curse he has been living with for the last forty years. The wizard says, "Maybe, but you will have to tell me the exact words that were used to put the curse on you."

The old man says without hesitation, "I now pronounce you man and wife."

There are two reasons why it is so hard to solve a redneck murder. One, the DNA all matches, and two, there are no dental records.

A blonde calls the airlines and asks, "Can you tell me how long it will take to fly from San Francisco to New York?"
The agent replies, "Just a minute..."
"Thank you," the blonde says, and she hangs up.

Two Mexican detectives were investigating the murder of Juan Gonzales. "How was he killed?" asked the one detective.
"With a golf gun," the other replied.
"A golf gun? What is a golf gun?"
"I don't know, but it sure made a hole in Juan."

"My wife got me to believe in religion," Moe said to Joe.
Joe said, "Really?"
"Yeah. Until I married her I didn't believe in hell."

A man is recovering from surgery when the surgical nurse appears and inquires how he is feeling. "I'm okay. But I didn't like the four-letter-word the doctor used in surgery."
"What did he say?" asks the nurse.
"Oops."

While shopping for vacation clothes, my husband and I passed a display of bathing suits. It had been at least two years and twenty pounds since I had even considered buying a bathing suit, so I sought my husband's advice. "What do you think?" I asked. "Should I get a bikini or an all-in-one?"
"Better get the bikini," he replied. "You'll never get it all in one."
My husband is still in intensive care.

# Handle It

Checking his wallet for the necessary payment, an old biker walks up to the bar and beckons to the exceptionally attractive female bartender serving a group of farmers.

"Yes?" she says with a smile. "May I help you?"

"I was wondering," he whispers, "are you the young lady who gives the great hand jobs?"

"Yes," she smiles and purrs, "I sure am."

The man replies, "Well, wash your hands real good, because I want a cheeseburger."

# Bubba

A redneck from Alabama walked into a bank in New York City and asked for the loan officer. He told the loan officer that he was going to Bakersfield on business for two weeks and needed to borrow $5,000 but that he was not a depositor of the bank.

The bank officer told him that the bank would need some form of security for the loan, so the man handed over the keys to a new Ferrari. The car was parked on the street in front of the bank. The redneck produced the title and everything checked out. The loan officer agreed to hold the car as collateral for the loan and apologized for having to charge twelve percent interest.

Later, the bank's president and its officers all enjoyed a good laugh at the redneck from the south for using a $250,000 Ferrari as collateral for a $5,000 loan. An employee of the bank drove the Ferrari into the bank's private underground garage and parked it.

Two weeks later, the redneck returned and repaid the $5,000 and the interest of $23.07. The loan officer said, "Sir, we are happy to have your business and the transaction has worked out very nicely, but we are all a little puzzled. While you were away, we checked you out and found that you are a multimillionaire. What puzzles us is: why would you bother to borrow $5,000?"

The good 'ole Alabama boy replied, "Where else in New York City can I park my car for two weeks for only $23.07 and expect it to be there when I return?"

# New Orleans Crabs

A man boarded an airplane in New Orleans with a box of frozen crabs and asked a blonde female crew member to take care of the box for him. She took the box and promised to put it in the crew's refrigerator.

The passenger pointedly advised her that he was holding her personally responsible for the crabs staying frozen, and then he mentioned that he was a lawyer before he proceeded to rant at her about what would happen if she let them thaw out.

Needless to say, she was annoyed by his behavior.

Shortly before landing in New York, the flight attendant used the intercom to announce to the entire cabin, "Would the gentleman who gave me the crabs in New Orleans please raise your hand?"

Not one hand went up, so she took the crabs home and ate them that night.

# Gynecologist Assistant

A retired man goes into the job center in downtown Denver and sees a card advertising for a gynecologist's assistant. Interested, he goes to learn more. "Can I get some details?" he asks the clerk.

The clerk pulls up the file and says, "The job entails getting the ladies ready for the gynecologist. You have to help the women out of their clothes, lay them down, and carefully wash their private area so that they are ready for the doctor to give them their exam. There's an annual salary of $65,000, but you're going to have to go to Billings, Montana. That's about 555 miles from here."

"Good grief! Is that where the job is?" the man asks.

"No sir, that's where the end of the line is right now to apply."

# Good Golf Wife

An elderly couple were having dinner one evening when the husband reached across the table, took his wife's hand in his, and said, "Martha, soon we will be married fifty years, and there's something I have to know. In all of these fifty years have you ever been unfaithful to me?"

Martha replied, "Well, Henry, I will be honest with you. Yes, I've been unfaithful to you three times during these fifty years, but always for a good reason."

Henry was obviously shocked and hurt by his wife's confession, but said, "I never suspected. Tell me—what do you mean by a good reason?"

Martha said, "The first time was shortly after we were married, and we were about to lose our little house because we couldn't pay the mortgage. Do you remember that one evening I went to see the banker and the next day he notified you that the loan would be extended?"

Henry recalled the visit to the banker and said, "I can forgive you for that—you saved our home. What about the second time?"

Martha asked, "Do you remember when you were so sick, but we didn't have the money to pay for the heart surgery you needed? Well, I went to see the doctor one night and, if you recall, he did the surgery at no cost."

"I recall that," Henry said. "And you did it to save my life, so of course I can forgive you for that. Now tell me about the third time."

"All right," Martha said. "Do you remember when you ran for president of your golf club, and you needed seventy-three more votes?"

# Spaghetti

For two years a man was having an affair with an Italian woman. One night, she confided in him that she was pregnant. Not wanting to ruin his reputation or his marriage, he paid her a large sum of money to go to Italy and secretly have their child. He said he would pay child support until the child turned eighteen, as long as she would stay hidden.

The woman agreed, but asked how he would know when the baby was born. To keep the message discreet, he told her to simply mail him a postcard and write the word "Spaghetti" on the back. He would then arrange for the support payments to begin.

One day about nine months later, he came home to his confused wife. "Honey," she said, "you received a very strange postcard today."

"Oh, just give it to me and I'll explain later," he said.

The wife complied and watched as her husband read the card, turned white, and fainted. On the card was written:

"Spaghetti, Spaghetti, Spaghetti, Spaghetti, Spaghetti. Three with meatballs and two without. Send extra sauce."

# A New Bike

For his birthday, little Joe asked for a ten-speed bicycle. His father said, "Son, we'd give you one, but the mortgage on this house is $280,000 and your mother just lost her job. There's no way we can afford it."

The next day, the father saw little Joe heading out the front door with a suitcase. He asked, "Son, where are you going?"

Little Joe said, "I was walking past your room last night and heard you telling Mommy you were pulling out. Then I heard her tell you to wait because she was coming too. And I'll be damned if I'm staying here by myself with a $280,000 mortgage and no bike."

# Men's Health Study

The American government funded a study to see why the head of a man's penis is larger than the shaft. After one year and $180,000, they concluded that the reason the head of the penis is larger than the shaft is to give the man more pleasure during sex.

After the U.S. published the study, the French decided to do their own study. After $250,000 and three years of research, they concluded that the reason the head of a man's penis is larger than the shaft is to give the woman more pleasure during sex.

Australia, unsatisfied with these findings, conducted their own study. After two weeks, and a cost of around $75.46 and two cases of beer, they concluded that the reason the head of a man's penis is larger than the shaft is to keep a man's hand from flying off and hitting himself in the forehead.

# Southern Choke

Two hillbillies walk into a restaurant. While having a bite to eat, they talk about their moonshine operation. Suddenly, a woman eating a sandwich at a nearby table begins to cough. After a minute or so it becomes apparent that she is in real distress. One of the hillbillies looks at her and says, "Kin ya swallar?"

The woman shakes her head no. Then he asks, "Kin ya breathe?"

The woman begins to turn blue and shakes her head no. The hillbilly walks over to the woman, lifts up her dress, yanks down her drawers, and quickly gives her right butt cheek a lick with his tongue. The woman is so shocked that she has a violent spasm and the obstruction flies out of her mouth.

As she begins to breathe again, the hillbilly walks slowly back to his table. His partner says, "Ya know, I'd heerd of that there Hind Lick Maneuver, but I ain't niver seed nobody do it."

# Herding

A cowboy named Bud was overseeing his herd in a remote, mountainous pasture in California when suddenly a brand-new sports car advanced toward him out of a cloud of dust. The driver, a young man in an expensive suit, fancy tie, and dark sunglasses, leaned out of the window and asked the cowboy, "If I tell you exactly how many cows and calves you have in your herd, will you give me a calf?"

Bud looked at the yuppie, then looked at his peacefully grazing herd and calmly answered, "Sure, why not?"

The city slicker parked his car, whipped out his laptop computer, connected it to his cell phone, and surfed to a page on the Internet. He logged on to a GPS satellite to get an exact fix on his location, which he then fed to another satellite that scanned the area and captured the image as an ultra-high-resolution photo. The young man then opened the digital photo and exported it to an image processing facility in Hamburg, Germany.

Within seconds, he received an e-mail on his Palm Pilot, and after a few more minutes, he received another transmission.

Finally, he printed out a full color, 150-page report on his high-tech, miniaturized laser printer. Turning to the cowboy, the young man said, "You have exactly 1,586 cows and calves."

"That's right. Well, I guess you can take one of my calves," Bud said.

He watched as the yuppie selected one of the animals, and looked on with amusement as the young man attempted to stuff it into the trunk of his car.

Then Bud said, "Hey—if I can tell you exactly what your business is will you give me back my calf?"

The young man thought about it for a minute and then replied, "Okay, why not?"

"You're a Congressman for the U.S. government," Bud said.

"Wow! That is correct!" he answered in surprise. "But how did you guess that?"

"No guessing required," Bud answered. "You showed up here even though nobody called you. You want to get paid for an answer I already knew. You used millions of dollars' worth of equipment trying to show me how much smarter than me you are, and you don't know a thing about how working people make a living—or about cows, for that matter. Because this is a herd of sheep. Now give me back my dog."

# Two Woodpeckers

A Mexican woodpecker and a Canadian woodpecker were in Mexico arguing about which place had the toughest trees. The Mexican woodpecker claimed Mexico had a tree that no woodpecker could peck. The Canadian woodpecker accepted his challenge and promptly pecked a hole in the tree with no problem. The Mexican woodpecker was amazed.

The Canadian woodpecker then challenged the Mexican woodpecker to peck a tree in Canada that was absolutely too tough to get through. The Mexican woodpecker expressed confidence that he could do it and accepted the challenge. The two flew to Canada where the Mexican woodpecker successfully pecked the so-called "impeck-able" tree almost without breaking a sweat.

Both woodpeckers were now terribly confused. How was it that the Canadian woodpecker was able to peck the Mexican tree, and the Mexican woodpecker was able to peck the Canadian tree, yet neither was able to peck the tree in his own country?

After much woodpecker pondering, they both came to the same conclusion: Apparently your pecker gets harder when you're away from home.

# Hypnosis

A woman comes home and tells her husband, "Remember those headaches I've been having all these years? Well, they're gone."

"No more headaches?" the husband asks. "What happened?"

His wife replies, "Margie referred me to a hypnotist and he told me to stand in front of a mirror, stare at myself, and repeat, 'I do not have a headache. I do not have a headache. I do not have a headache.' Well, it worked! The headaches are all gone."

"That's wonderful," proclaims the husband. His wife then says, "You know, you haven't been exactly a ball of fire in the bedroom these last few years—why don't you go see the hypnotist and see if he can do anything for that?" Reluctantly, the husband agrees to try it.

Following his appointment, the husband comes home, rips off his clothes, picks up his wife, and carries her into the bedroom. He puts her on the bed and says, "Don't move, I'll be right back." He goes into the bathroom and comes back a few minutes later, jumps into bed, and makes passionate love to his wife like never before. His wife says, "Wow! That was wonderful!"

The husband says, "Don't move. I will be right back." He goes back into the bathroom, comes back, and round two is even better than the first time. The wife sits up and her head is spinning. "Oh my god!" she says breathlessly.

Her husband again says, "Don't move—I'll be right back."

With that, he goes back in the bathroom, but this time his wife quietly follows him in there. In the bathroom, she sees him standing at the mirror saying, "She's not my wife. She's not my wife. She's not my wife. She's not my wife."

His funeral service will be held on Saturday.

# Italian Paramedics

Vinny and Sal are out in the woods hunting when suddenly Sal grabs his chest and falls to the ground. He doesn't seem to be breathing, and his eyes have rolled back in his head.

Vinny whips out his cell phone and calls 911. He gasps to the operator, "I think Sal is dead! What should I do?"

The operator says in a calm, soothing voice, "Just take it easy and follow my instructions. First, let's make sure he's dead."

There is a silence, and then a loud gunshot is heard. Vinny's voice comes back on the line, "Okay, now what?"

# Getting a Dog

A woman was leaving a convenience store with her morning coffee when she noticed a most unusual funeral procession approaching the nearby cemetery. A long black hearse was followed by a second long black hearse about fifty feet behind. Behind the second hearse was a solitary woman walking a pit bull dog on a leash. Behind her were two hundred women walking single file.

The woman leaving the store couldn't bear the curiosity. She respectfully approached the woman walking the dog and said, "I am sorry for your loss, and I know now is a bad time to disturb you, but I've never seen a funeral like this one. Whose funeral is it?"

The woman replied, "Well, that first hearse is for my husband."

"What happened to him?"

The woman replied, "My dog attacked and killed him."

The first woman inquired further, "Well, who is in the second hearse?"

"His mistress. She tried to help my husband, so the dog turned on her, too."

A poignant and thoughtful moment of silence passed between the two women. "Can I borrow the dog?" the woman asked.

"Get in line," the widow answered.

# Vocabulary

Adult - A person who has stopped growing at both ends and is now growing in the middle.

Beauty Parlor - A place where women curl up and dye.

Cannibal - Someone who is fed up with people.

Chicken - The only animal you eat before they are born and after they are dead.

Committee - A body that keeps minutes and wastes hours.

Dust - Mud with the juice squeezed out.

Egotist - Someone who is usually me-deep in conversation.

Gossip - A person who will never tell a lie, but only if the truth will do more damage.

Handkerchief - Cold storage.

Inflation - Cutting money in half without damaging the paper.

Mosquito - An insect that makes you appreciate flies.

Raisin - A grape with a sunburn.

Secret - Something you tell to one person at a time.

Skeleton - A bunch of bones with the person scraped off.

Toothache - A pain that drives you to extraction.

Tomorrow - One of the greatest labor-saving devices of today.

Yawn - An honest opinion openly expressed.

Wrinkles - Something only other people have. You have character lines.

# Boys and Girls

A little girl and a little boy were playing. The boy said to the girl, "I bet I have something that you don't have."

So he pulled up his shirt and pointed to his belly button. The little girl pulled up her shirt and pointed to her own belly button and said, "Oh, no you don't."

"I bet you don't have two of these," the little boy continued, as he pulled his shirt up a little higher and pointed to his nipples.

The little girl did the same and said, "Oh, yes I do," as she pointed to her own.

The little boy wouldn't give up, so he pulled down his pants and pointed to his penis. The little girl pulled her pants down and, naturally, didn't see a penis and she ran home crying.

The next day the little boy saw the little girl humming and skipping along. "What are you so happy about? You don't even have one of these," he said to her as he pointed to his crotch.

The little girl, now secure, points to her "private" and said, "My mommy said that as long as I have one of THESE, I can have as many of THOSE as I want."

# Children

When my grandson Billy and I entered our vacation cabin, we kept the lights off until we were inside to keep from attracting pesky insects. Still, a few fireflies followed us in. Noticing them before I did, Billy whispered, "It's no use, Grandpa. The mosquitoes are coming after us with flashlights."

After putting her child to bed, a mother changed into old slacks and a droopy blouse and proceeded to wash her hair. As she heard the children getting more and more rambunctious, her patience grew thin. At last she threw the towel around her head and stormed into their room, putting them back to bed with stern warnings. As she left the room, she heard her three-year-old say with a trembling voice, "What was that?"

A mother was telling her little girl what her own childhood was like. She said she use to skate outside on a pond. She had a swing made from a tire that hung from a tree in her front yard. She rode her pony. They picked wild raspberries in the woods. The little girl was wide-eyed, taking it all in.
    At last she said, "I sure wish I'd gotten to know you sooner."

My grandson was visiting one day when he asked, "Grandma, do you know how you and God are alike?"
    I mentally polished my halo as I asked, "No. How are we alike?"
    "You're both really old," he answered.

A little girl was diligently pounding away on her father's

word processor. She told him she was writing a story. "What's it about?" the father asked.

"I don't know," she replied. "I can't read."

I wasn't sure if my granddaughter had learned her colors yet, so I decided to test her. I would point to things and ask her what color it was. She would tell me, and was always correct. It was fun for me so I continued. Finally, as she headed for the front door, she said sassily, "Grandma, I think you should try figuring some of these out for yourself."

When a man's grandson asked him how old he was, teasingly the man replied, "I'm not sure."

"Look in your underwear, Grandpa," the boy advised. "Mine says I'm four."

A second-grader came home from school and said to her mother, "Mom, guess what? We learned how to make babies today."

The mother, more than a little surprised, tried to keep her cool. "That's interesting," she said. "How do you make babies?"

"It's simple," the girl replied. "You just have to change the Y to IES."

# Not My Brother

An unmarried pregnant woman got in a car accident and fell into a deep coma. Asleep for nearly six months, when she woke up and saw that she was no longer pregnant she frantically asked the doctor about the baby.

The doctor replied, "Congratulations, you had twins—a boy and a girl. Your brother heard about the accident and since he was the closest relative we could find, we had him name the babies."

The woman thinks to herself, *No, not my brother—he is an idiot.* "Well, what's the girl's name?" she asked the doctor.

"Denise," he said.

"Wow, that's not a bad name. I like it. What's the boy's name?"

"Denephew."

# Replacing Nursing Homes

With the average cost of a room in a nursing home reaching over $200 a day, you need to know there is a better way.

It has been proven that one can get a nice room at a reputable hotel for under $100. That leaves $100 a day for beer, room service, laundry, gratuities, and special TV movies. Plus most hotels have a swimming pool, a workout room, a lounge, washer and dryer, etc. And they even supply free toothpaste, razors, shampoo, and soap. Sometimes at the front desk you can even get a toothbrush if you tell them you forgot yours.

To make it even more economical, many offer a free breakfast with fresh waffles you make yourself. For lunch and dinner, you usually have to walk next door. But that's not bad, because it gives you a change of scenery. And although there may be a bit of a wait to get the first floor rooms, that's okay, because sometimes it takes months to get into decent nursing homes.

There is plenty of transportation, too, with no one to tell you what to do. You can jump on the senior bus, a church bus, or just grab a cab. For a real change of pace, you can always take the airport bus and eat at one of its many cafes and then when you're done, just pop on the shuttle back.

Not to mention that hotel security is great. This way, if you happen to drop off, at least someone will notice; and should by chance you fall and seriously injure yourself, at least you can always sue. What more could you ask for?

As a bonus, they all have AARP and senior discounts.

# Digging Ditches

A guy stopped at a gas station and after filling his tank, he grabbed a soft drink and paid the bill. He stood by his car drinking a soda and watching a couple of men working along the roadside. One man would dig a hole two or three feet deep and then move on. The other man would then come along behind him and fill in the hole. While one was digging a hole, the other was filling in the previous hole. The men worked right past the guy with the cola and went on down the road.

"I can't understand this," said the man, tossing the can into a trash container and heading down the road toward them.

"Hold it, hold it!" he called to the men. "Can you tell me what's going on here with all this digging and refilling?"

"Well, we work for the government, and we're just doing our job," one man said.

"But one of you is digging a hole and the other is filling it. You're not accomplishing anything! Aren't you just wasting taxpayers' money?"

"You don't understand, mister," the worker said, leaning on his shovel and wiping his brow. "Normally there's three of us: me, Elmer, and Leroy. I dig the hole, Elmer sticks in the tree, and then Leroy puts the dirt back. Elmer's job's been cut, so now it's just me and Leroy."

# Living to Be Ninety

An older woman recently picked a new primary care physician. After two visits and comprehensive lab tests, he said she was doing "fairly well" for her age. A little concerned about his comment, she couldn't resist asking him, "Do you think I'll live to be ninety?"

He asked, "Well, do you smoke or drink?"

"Oh, no," she replied. "Not for over twenty years."

"Do you eat red meat and greasy foods?"

"No. I have always maintained a healthy diet."

"Do you spend a lot of time in the sun?" he asked.

"No, I don't," she replied.

"Do you gamble, drive fast cars, or fool around?"

"No," she said. "I've never been that way."

The doctor looked at the woman and said, "Well, then, why in the hell would you *want* to live to be ninety?"

# Oh, Really

He said, "What have you done with all the grocery money I gave you?"

She said, "Turn sideways and look in the mirror."

What do you call an intelligent, good looking, sensitive man?
A rumor.

One day my housework-challenged husband decided to wash his sweatshirt. Seconds after he stepped into the laundry room, he shouted, "What setting do I use on the washing machine?"

"What does your shirt say?"

He yelled back, "University of Oklahoma."

A man and his wife, now in their sixties, were celebrating their fortieth wedding anniversary. On their special day a good fairy came to them and said that because they had been such a devoted couple she was going to grant them each one very special wish.

The wife wished for a trip around the world with her husband. Whoosh! Immediately she had airline and cruise tickets in her hand.

The man wished for a female companion thirty years younger. Whoosh! Immediately he turned ninety.

A woman's perfect breakfast:
She is sitting at the table with her gourmet coffee.
Her son is on the cover of the Wheaties box.

Her daughter is on the cover of *Business Week* magazine.
Her boyfriend is on the cover of *Playgirl* magazine.
And her husband is on the back of a milk carton.

# Interview

An office manager was given the task of hiring an individual to fill a job opening. After sorting through a stack of resumes he found four people who were equally qualified. He decided to call them all in and ask them a single question. Their answer would determine which of them he would hire.

The day came and the four sat around the conference table. Addressing the man to his right, the interviewer asked, "What is the fastest thing you know of?"

The first man replied, "A thought. It pops into your head, there is no forewarning that it is on its way, it's just there. A thought is the fastest thing I know of."

"That's very good," replied the interviewer. "And now you, sir?" he asked the second man.

"Hmmm, let me see. A blink. It comes and goes, and you don't know it ever happened. A blink is the fastest thing I know of."

"Excellent," the interviewer said. "The blink of an eye. That's a very popular metaphor for speed."

The third man was contemplating his reply and offered: "Well, out at my dad's ranch, you step out of the house and on the wall there's a light switch. When you flip that switch, way out across the pasture the light in the barn comes on in an instant. Turning on a light is the fastest thing I can think of."

The interviewer was very impressed with the third prospect's answer, and thought he had found his man. "It's hard to beat the speed of light," he said.

Turning to the fourth man, he again posed the question. "After hearing the three previous answers, it's obvious to me that the fastest thing I know of is diarrhea."

"What?" said the interviewer, stunned by the response.

"I can explain," said the fourth man. "You see, the other day I wasn't feeling so well and I ran for the bathroom. But, before I could think, blink, or turn on the light, I'd already shit my pants."

He got the job.

# Rewind

I walked into a hair salon with my husband and three kids in tow and asked loudly, "How much do you charge for a shampoo and blow job?"

I thought about it for a minute, what I had just asked, before I turned around and walked out. My husband didn't say a word. He obviously knew better.

I was at a golf store comparing different kinds of golf balls; I was unhappy with the women's type I had been using. After browsing for several minutes, I was approached by one of the good-looking gentlemen who worked at the store. He asked if he could help me. Without thinking, I looked at him and said, "I think I like playing with men's balls better."

While in line at the bank one afternoon, my toddler decided to release some pent-up energy and ran amok. I was finally able to grab hold of her arm after receiving looks of disgust and annoyance from other patrons. I told her that if she didn't start behaving immediately, she would be punished.

To my horror, she looked me in the eye and said in a voice just as threatening, "If you don't take your hands off me right now, I am going to tell Grandma that I saw you kissing Daddy's 'pee-pee' last night."

The silence was deafening after this enlightening exchange. Even the tellers stopped what they were doing. I mustered up the last of my dignity and walked out the door of the bank with my daughter in tow. The last thing I heard when the door closed behind me was screams of laughter.

My three-year-old son had a lot of problems with potty training, and I was on him constantly. One day we stopped at a fast food restaurant for a quick lunch between errands. It was very busy, with a full dining room. While enjoying our meal, I smelled something funny, so of course I checked my seven-month-old daughter, but she was clean. Then, realizing that my son had not asked to go potty in a while, I asked him if he needed to go. He said, "No."

I kept thinking, *Oh, Lord, that child has had an accident, and I don't have any extra clothes with me.* Then I said, "Are you sure you didn't have an accident?"

"No," he replied.

I just knew that he must have pooped his pants because the smell was getting worse. So I asked one more time, "Son, are you sure you didn't have an accident?"

This time he jumped up, yanked down his pants, bent over and spread his cheeks, and yelled, "See mom, it's just farts!"

While at least thirty people nearly choked to death on their food from laughing, he calmly pulled up his pants and sat down. One older couple made me feel a little better by thanking me for the best laugh they'd had in a long time.

One day a television news station hired a new female anchor. During the weather forecast that day, it was predicted that the area would get a good amount of snow before morning. The next day, after it did not snow at all, she turned to the weatherman and asked, "So, where's that eight inches you promised me last night?"

Not only did the weatherman have to leave the set, but half the crew did, too, because they were laughing so hard.

# Sniffer

A man is sitting on an airplane, which is about to take off, when another man with a Labrador Retriever occupies the two empty seats behind him. The Lab is situated in the middle. The first man is looking back quizzically at the dog when the second man explains that he works for the airline. The airline representative says, "Don't mind Sniffer. He is a sniffing dog— the best there is. I'll show you once we get airborne, when I put him to work."

The plane takes off and levels out when the handler says to the first man, "Watch this."

He tells the dog, "Search."

Sniffer jumps down, walks past rows of seats, and sits next to a woman for a few seconds. He then returns to his handler and puts his paw on the man's arm.

"Good boy," he says.

The airline official turns to the passenger and explains, "That woman is in possession of marijuana so I'm taking note of her seat number for the police, who will apprehend her on our arrival."

"Fantastic," replies the first man.

Once again, Sniffer is sent to search the aisle. The dog sniffs about, sits down beside a man for a few seconds, returns to his handler, and places two paws on the man's arm. The airline official says, "That man is carrying cocaine. So again, I'm making note of the seat number."

"I like it," the first man says.

A third time the rep sends Sniffer to search the aisle. Sniffer goes up and down the plane and after a while sits down next to someone. He then comes racing back, jumps up onto his seat, and poops all over the place. The first man is disgusted by this behavior from a supposedly well-trained sniffing dog. He asks, "What's going on?"

The handler nervously replies, "He just found a bomb."

# Following Directions

Miss Bea, the church organist, was in her eighties and had never been married. She was much admired for her sweetness and kindness to all. The pastor came to call on her one afternoon. She welcomed him to her Victorian parlor and invited him to have a seat while she prepared some tea. As he sat facing her old pump organ, the young minister noticed a cut glass bowl filled with water sitting on top of it. Floating in the water was a condom, of all things. Imagine the reverend's shock and surprise. Imagine his curiosity.

When Miss Bea returned with the tea and cookies, they began to chat. The pastor tried to stifle his curiosity about the bowl of water and its strange floater, but soon it got the better of him and he could resist no longer. "Miss Bea," he said, pointing to the bowl, "I wonder if you would tell me about this?"

"Oh, yes," she replied, "Isn't it wonderful?

I was walking downtown last spring and I found this little package on the ground. The directions said to put it on the organ, keep it wet, and it would prevent disease. And you know, I haven't had a cold all winter."

# The Fire Engine

A firefighter was working on an engine outside the station when he noticed a little girl pulling a little red wagon with toy ladders hung off the side and a garden hose tightly coiled in the middle.

The girl was wearing a firefighter's helmet, and the wagon was tied to a dog and a cat.

The fireman walked over to take a closer look. "That sure is a nice fire truck," the firefighter said with admiration.

"Thanks," the little girl said.

The firefighter looked a little closer and noticed the girl had tied the wagon to the dog's collar and the cat's testicles. "Little partner," he said, "I don't want to tell you how to run your fire truck, but if you were to tie the rope around the cat's collar, I think you could go faster."

The little girl replied, "You're probably right, but then I wouldn't have a siren."

# 'Twas the Night of Thanksgiving

'Twas the night of Thanksgiving, but I just couldn't sleep.
I tried counting backwards, I tried counting sheep.
The leftovers beckoned, the dark meat and white,
But I fought the temptation with all of my might.
Tossing and turning with anticipation,
The thought of a snack became infatuation.
So I raced to the kitchen, flung open the door,
And gazed at the fridge, full of goodies galore.
I gobbled up turkey and buttered potatoes,
Pickles and carrots, beans and tomatoes.
I felt myself swelling so plump and so round,
'Til all of a sudden, I rose off the ground.
I crashed through the ceiling, floated into the sky
With a mouthful of pudding, a handful of pie.
But I managed to yell as I soared past the trees,
"Happy eating to all! Pass the cranberries, please!"
May your stuffing be tasty, your turkey be plump,
Your potatoes 'n gravy have nary a lump.
May your yams be delicious, your pies take the prize.
May your Thanksgiving dinner stay off of your thighs.

# Cannibals

"You are all part of our team now," said the Human Resources representative during a welcoming briefing. "You get all the usual benefits and you can go to the cafeteria for something to eat, but please do not eat any of the employees."

The cannibals promised that they would not.

Four weeks later, their boss remarked, "You're all working very hard, and I am very satisfied with you. However, one of our secretaries has disappeared. Do any of you know what happened to her?"

The cannibals all shook their heads "No."

After the boss left, the leader of the cannibals shouted, "You fools! For four weeks we've been eating managers and no one noticed anything. But noooo, you had to go eat someone important."

# Thinking Back

A woman awakens during the night to find her husband is not in bed. She puts on her robe and goes downstairs to look for him. She finds him sitting at the kitchen table with a cup of coffee in front of him. He appears to be in deep thought, just staring at the wall. She watches as he wipes a tear from his eye and takes a sip of his coffee.

"What's the matter, dear?" she whispers as she steps into the room. "Why are you down here at this time of night?"

The husband looks up from his coffee cup and says, "Do you remember twenty years ago when we were dating, and you were only sixteen?" he asks solemnly.

"Yes, I do," she answers.

The husband pauses. The words are not coming easily. "Do you remember when your father caught us in the back seat of my car?"

"Yes, I remember," says the wife, lowering herself into a chair beside him.

The husband continues, "Do you remember when he shoved his shotgun in my face and said I either had to marry you or he'd send me to jail for twenty years?"

"Yes, I remember that too," she replies softly.

He wipes another tear from his cheek and says, "I would have gotten out today."

# The Parrot

A young man received a parrot as a gift. The parrot had a bad disposition and an even worse vocabulary. Every utterance from the bird's mouth was rude, obnoxious, and laced with profanity. The man tried and tried to change the bird's speech by consistently saying only polite words, playing soft music, and doing anything else he could think of to "clean up" the bird's language. Finally he was fed up and he yelled at the parrot. The parrot yelled back. The man shook the parrot and the bird got angrier and even ruder. The man, in desperation, threw up his hands, grabbed the parrot and put him in the freezer. For a few minutes the parrot squawked and kicked and screamed.

Then suddenly there was total quiet. Not a peep was heard for over a minute. Fearing he had hurt his pet, he quickly opened the door to the freezer. The parrot calmly stepped out onto his owner's outstretched arm and said, "I believe I may have offended you with my rude language and actions. I'm sincerely remorseful for my inappropriate transgressions, and I fully intend to do everything I can to correct my horrible behavior."

The man was stunned at the change in the bird's attitude. As he was about to ask the parrot what had caused such a dramatic change in his behavior, the bird continued, "May I ask what the turkey did?"

# I Promised

There was a man who had worked all of his life and saved all his money. He was a real miser. He loved money more than just about anything. Just before he died, he said to his wife, "Now listen—when I go, I want you to take all my money and place it in the casket with me. I want to take my money to the afterlife."

So he got his wife to promise him with all her heart that when he died she would put all his money in the casket with him.

Well, one day he did die. At the memorial service, he was stretched out in the casket and the wife was sitting in the back of the funeral parlor next to her closest friend. When they finished the ceremony, just before the casket was closed the widow said, "Wait—just a minute."

She approached the casket, carrying a shoebox with her. She placed the box inside, next to her late husband. Then the undertaker locked the casket down and rolled it away.

Her friend said, "I hope you weren't crazy enough to put all his money in there."

She answered, "Yes, I promised. I'm a good Christian. I can't lie. I promised him that I was going to put the money in the casket with him."

"You mean to tell me you put every cent of his money in the casket with him?"

"I sure did," said the wife. "I got it all together, put it into my account, and I wrote him a check."

# Banking

A little old lady went into the Bank of Canada one day, carrying a bag of money. She insisted that she speak to the president of the bank to open a savings account because, she said, "It's a lot of money."

After much hemming and hawing, the bank staff finally ushered her into the president's office. The president then asked her how much she would like to deposit. She replied, "$165,000" and she dumped the cash out of her bag onto his desk.

The president was, of course, curious as to how she came by all this cash, so he asked her, "Ma'am, I'm surprised you're carrying so much cash around. Where did you get this money?"

The old lady answered, "I make bets."

The president then asked, "Bets? What kind of bets?"

"Well, for example, I'll bet you $25,000 that your balls are square," she said.

"Ha," laughed the president, "that's a stupid bet. You can't win that kind of bet."

The old lady challenged, "So, would you like to take my bet?"

"Sure," the president said. "I'll bet you $25,000 that my balls are not square."

The little old lady then said, "Okay, but since there is a lot of money involved, may I bring my lawyer with me tomorrow at 10:00 a.m. as a witness?"

"Sure," replied the confident president.

That night the president got very nervous about the bet and spent a long time in front of a mirror checking his balls, turning them from side to side, again and again. He thoroughly checked them out until he was sure there was absolutely no way his balls were square and that he would win the bet.

The next morning, at precisely 10:00 a.m., the little old lady appeared at the bank with her lawyer. She introduced her lawyer to the president and in his office repeated the bet, "$25,000 says the president's balls are square."

The president agreed to the bet again and the old lady asked him to drop his pants so they could all see. The president did. The little old lady peered closely at his balls and then asked if she could feel them.

"Well, okay," the president said, "$25,000 is a lot of money, so I guess you should be absolutely sure."

Just then, he noticed that the lawyer was quietly banging his head against the wall. The bank president asked the old lady, "What the hell is wrong with your lawyer?"

She replied, "Nothing, except I bet him $100,000 that at 10:00 a.m. today I'd have the Bank of Canada's president's balls in my hand."

# Neighborly Chat

A farmer got in his pickup, drove several miles to a neighboring farm, and knocked on the farmhouse door. A young boy about twelve years old opened the door. "Is your pa home?" the farmer asked.

"No, sir, he ain't. He went into town."

"Well," the farmer said, "is your ma home?"

"No, sir. She ain't home either," the boy replied. "She went into town with my pa."

"How about your brother Lloyd? Is he here?"

"No. He went with Ma and Pa."

The farmer stood there for a few minutes, shifted from one foot to another, and mumbled to himself. "Is there anything I can do for you?" the boy asked politely. "I know where all the tools are, if you want to borrow something. Or maybe I could take a message for my pa."

"Well," said the farmer uncomfortably, "I really wanted to talk to your pa. It's about your brother Lloyd getting my daughter pregnant."

The boy thought for a moment. "You will have to talk to Pa about that," he finally conceded. "If it helps you any, I know that Pa charges $50 for the bull and $25 for the boar hog, but I really don't know how much he gets for Lloyd."

# Valuable Lesson

I was happy. My girlfriend and I had been dating for over a year, so we decided to get married. My parents helped us in every way and even my friends encouraged me. And my girlfriend— she was a dream. There was only one thing that bothered me, and very much indeed. That one thing was my girlfriend's younger sister. My prospective sister-in-law was twenty years old and wore tight miniskirts and low-cut blouses. She would regularly bend over when near me, revealing many pleasant views of her breasts. It had to be deliberate—she never did it when she was near anyone else.

One day, little sister called and asked me to come over and check the wedding invitations. She was alone when I arrived. She whispered to me that soon I was to be married and she had feelings and desires for me that she couldn't overcome and didn't really want to overcome. She told me that she wanted to make love to me just once before I got married and committed my life to her sister. I was in total shock and couldn't say a word. She said, "I'm going upstairs to my bedroom so if you want to go ahead with it, just come up and get me."

I was stunned. I was frozen in shock as I watched her go up the stairs. When she reached the top she pulled down her panties and threw them down the stairs at me. I stood there for a moment, then turned and went straight to the front door. I opened the door and stepped out of the house and walked straight to my car. My future father-in-law was standing outside. With tears in his eyes, he hugged me and said, "We are very happy that you have passed our little test. We couldn't ask for a better man for our daughter. Welcome to the family."

The young man thought to himself, *It's a good thing I keep my condoms in the car.*

# Preaching to the Bears

A Catholic priest, a Pentecostal preacher, and a rabbi would get together two or three times a week for coffee and to talk shop. One day, someone made the comment that preaching to people isn't really all that hard. A real challenge would be to preach to a bear.

One thing led to another and they decided to do a seven-day experiment. They would all go out into the woods, find a bear, preach to it, and attempt to convert it.

Seven days later, they all wound up in the hospital together and began to discuss their experiences. Father Flannery, who had his arm in a sling, was on crutches, and had various bandages, went first. "Well," he said, "I went into the woods to find a bear. And when I found him I began to read to him from the catechism. Well, that bear wanted nothing to do with me and began to slap me. So I quickly grabbed my holy water, sprinkled him, and— Holy Mary, Mother of God—he became gentle as a lamb. The bishop is coming out next week to give him communion and confirmation."

Reverend Billy Bob spoke next. He was in a wheelchair, with an arm and both legs in casts, and an IV drip. In his best fire-and-brimstone oratory he proclaimed, "Well, brothers, you know that we don't sprinkle, we dunk. I went out and I found me a bear. And then I began to read to him from God's Holy Word. But that bear wanted nothing to do with me. So I took hold of him and we began to wrestle. We wrestled down one hill, up another, and down another, until we came to a crick. So I quickly dunked him and baptized his hairy soul. And just like you said, he became gentle as a lamb. We spent the rest of the week in fellowship, feasting on God's Holy Word and praising Jesus."

They both looked down at the rabbi, who was lying in a hospital bed. He was in a body cast and traction, with IVs and monitors running in and out of him. He was in bad shape. The rabbi looked up and said, "Oy! You fellows don't know what trouble is until you try to circumcise one of those hairy buggers."

# Getting into Heaven

After a long illness, a woman died and arrived at the gates of Heaven. While she was waiting for Saint Peter to greet her, she peeked through the gates and saw a beautiful banquet table. Sitting all around it were her parents and all the other people she loved who had died before her. They saw her and began calling greetings to her. "Hello! How are you? We've been waiting for you. Good to see you."

When Saint Peter came by, the woman said to him, "This is such a wonderful place. How do I get in?"

"You have to spell a word," Saint Peter told her.

"Which word?" the woman asked.

"Love."

The woman correctly spelled it, and Saint Peter welcomed her to Heaven.

About six months later, Saint Peter came to the woman and asked her to watch the gates for him that day. While the woman was standing guard, her husband arrived. "I'm surprised to see you," the woman said. "How have you been?"

"Oh, I've been doing pretty well since you died," her husband told her. "I married the beautiful young nurse who took care of you while you were ill. Then I won the lottery, sold the little house you and I lived in, and bought a big mansion. My new wife and I traveled all around the world. We were on vacation and I went water-skiing today. I fell, the ski hit my head, and here I am. How do I get in?"

"You have to spell a word," the woman told him.

"Which word?" her husband asked.

"Czechoslovakia."

# Preacher's Wife

A man stopped by the pastor's home and asked to see his wife. She was widely known to be a charitable woman. "Ma'am," he said in a broken, teary voice, "I wish to draw your attention to a family in desperate need. You see, the father has died, the mother is too ill to work, and the nine children are starving. What's worse, they are about to be evicted unless someone pays their rent of $400."

"Oh," exclaimed the preacher's wife, "how awful! Tell me, sir, who are you?"

Delicately taking a handkerchief to his eyes to dab the tears away, the man explained, "I'm the landlord."

# Nosey

I was barely sitting down when I heard a voice from the bathroom stall next to me say, "Hi, how are you?"

I'm not the type to start a conversation in the restroom, and I don't know what got into me, but I answered, somewhat embarrassed, "Just fine, thanks."

And the other person says, "So what are you up to?"

What kind of question is that? At that point, I'm thinking, *This is too bizarre!* So I say, "Uhhh, I'm like you, just traveling."

At this point I am trying to get out as fast as I can when I hear another question: "Can I come over?"

Okay, this question is just too weird for me, but I figure I could just be polite and end the conversation. I tell him, "No, I'm a little busy right now."

Then I hear the person say nervously, "Listen I'll call you back. There is an idiot in the other stall who keeps answering my questions."

# I'll Feed You

One afternoon, a wealthy lawyer was driving in his limousine when he saw two men along the roadside, eating grass. Disturbed by the sight, he ordered his driver to stop and he got out to investigate. He asked one man, "Why are you eating grass?"

"We don't have any money for food," the poor man replied. "We have to eat grass."

"Well, then, you can come home with me to my house and I'll feed you," the lawyer said.

"But sir, I have a wife and two children with me. They are over there, under the tree."

"Bring them along," the lawyer replied. Turning to the other poor man, he added, "You can come with us, too."

The second man then stated in a pitiful voice, "But sir, I also have a wife and six children with me."

"Bring them all," the lawyer answered.

They all entered the car, which was no easy task even for a car as large as the limousine. Once underway, one of the poor fellows turned to the lawyer and said, "Sir, you are too kind. Thank you for taking all of us with you."

The lawyer replied, "Glad to do it. You'll really love my place—the grass is almost a foot high."

# Blonde Officer

A blonde female police officer was working radar one afternoon. A blonde female driver flew through the speed trap at 85 mph and was pulled over. The officer asked to see the motorist's driver's license. She started rooting around through her purse and finally confessed that she didn't know what it looked like.

The officer told her that it had her picture on it. The driver finally found a small mirror in the bottom of her purse. When she stared at it, she saw her "picture." She thought that this was probably what the officer was looking for, so she handed the mirror to her.

The officer stared at it intently for a minute. She then turned to the driver and said, "You're free to go. If I had known you were a police officer I wouldn't have pulled you over in the first place."

# Sex of a Fly

A woman walked into the kitchen to find her husband stalking around with a fly swatter. "What are you doing?" she asked.

"Hunting flies," he answered.

"Kill any?" she asked.

"Yep. Three males and two females," he replied.

Intrigued, she asked, "How can you tell them apart?"

He responded, "Three were on a beer can and two were on the phone."

# Little Boy Choking

A father walks into a bookstore with his young son. The boy is holding a quarter. Suddenly the boy starts choking and going blue in the face. The father realizes the boy has swallowed the quarter, and starts to panic. He shouts for help.

A well-dressed, attractive, serious-looking woman in a blue business suit is sitting at the coffee bar reading a newspaper. At the sound of the commotion, she looks up, puts her coffee cup down, neatly folds her newspaper, and places it on the counter. She then gets up from her seat and makes her way, unhurried, across the bookstore.

Reaching the boy, the woman carefully drops his pants, takes hold of the boy's testicles, and starts to squeeze and twist, gently at first and then ever so firmly. After a few seconds, the boy convulses violently and coughs up the quarter, which the woman deftly catches in her free hand.

Releasing the boy's testicles, the woman hands the coin to the father and walks back to her seat at the coffee bar without saying a word.

As soon as the father is sure that his son has suffered no ill effects he rushes over to the woman and starts thanking her. He says, "I've never seen anyone do anything like that before. It was FANTASTIC. Are you a doctor?"

"No," the woman replied. "Divorce attorney."

# Modern Technology

Three women—one German, one Japanese, and a hillbilly—were sitting naked in a sauna. Suddenly there was a beeping sound. The German lady pressed her forearm and the beep stopped. The others looked at her questioningly. "That was my pager," she said. "I have a microchip under the skin of my arm."

A few minutes later, a phone rang. The Japanese woman lifted her palm to her ear. When she finished, she explained, "That was my mobile phone. I have a microchip in my hand."

The hillbilly woman felt decidedly low tech. Not to be outdone, she decided she too had to do something just as impressive. She stepped out of the sauna and went to the bathroom. She returned with a piece of toilet paper hanging from the crack of her butt. The others raised their eyebrows and stared at her. The hillbilly woman finally said, "Well, will you look at that, I'm getting a fax."

# Remedy

There was a guy who always went out drinking with his friends. He would always come home very late. One night at the bar he told his friends his secret for being able to sneak in late. "When I walk in the house, before my wife can say anything, I lay her down, take off her panties, and give her the best oral sex she's ever had until she has such an orgasm that she falls into a deep sleep. Then I wash up and go to bed. By morning she is so pleased she doesn't care what time I came home."

One of his friends thought this was a great idea. So he stayed out late, came home, sneaked into the bedroom, gave his wife the best oral sex she had ever had and went to wash up. His wife walked into the bathroom, obviously upset that he was home so late.

"Hey, why aren't you sleeping?" he asked.

"I was, but I came in to tell you that we've got to sleep on the couch tonight because my mother is sleeping in our room."

# Because I'm Blonde?

A girl came home from school one day. "Mommy, Mommy!" she yelled. "We were counting today, and all the other kids could only count to four, but I counted to ten! See? 1, 2, 3, 4, 5, 6, 7, 8, 9, 10."

"Very good," her mother said.

"Is it because I'm blonde, Mommy?"

"Yes, honey, it's because you're blonde."

The next day the girl came skipping home from school. "Mommy, Mommy!" she yelled. "We were saying our alphabet today, and all the other kids could only say it to D, but I said it to G! See? A, B, C, D, E, F, G!"

"Very good," said her mother.

"Is it because I'm blonde, Mommy?"

"Yes, honey, it's because you're blonde."

The next day the girl came skipping home from school. "Mommy, Mommy!" she yelled. "We were in gym class today and when we showered, all the other girls had flat chests, but I have these," she said as she lifted her tank top up to reveal a pair of 36Cs.

"Very good," said the embarrassed mother.

"Is it because I'm blonde, Mommy?"

"No, honey, it is because you're 25."

# Pass Him

A first-grade teacher was constantly pestered by one of her students. The teacher asked Johnny, "What is your problem?"

Johnny answered, "My sister is in the third grade, and I am smarter than she is. I think I should be in the third grade, too."

The teacher had enough. She took Johnny to the principal's office. While Johnny waited in the outer office, the teacher explained the situation.

The principal told the teacher he would give the boy a test. If he failed to answer any of the questions, Johnny would be compelled to go back to first grade and behave. She agreed.

Johnny was brought into the office and the conditions were explained to him. He agreed to take the test. The principal asked, "What is three times three?"

Johnny answered, "Nine."

"What is six times six?"

Johnny answered, "Thirty-six."

And so it went with every question the principal thought a third-grader should know. The teacher then said to the principal, "Let me ask him some questions."

The principal and Johnny agreed. The teacher asked, "What does a cow have four of that I only have two of?"

Johnny answered, "Legs."

"What is in your pants that you have but I don't?"

The principal wondered, *Why would she ask such a question?*

Johnny replied, "Pockets."

"What does a dog do that a man steps into?"

Johnny said, "Pants."

The teacher asked, "What starts with a C, ends with a T, is

hairy, oval, delicious, and contains thin, whitish liquid?"

Johnny said, "Coconut."

The principal sat forward with his mouth hanging open. The teacher continued. "What goes in hard and pink then comes out soft and sticky?"

The principal began to tremble. Johnny said, "Bubble gum."

The teacher continued. "What does a man do standing up, a woman do sitting down, and a dog do on three legs?"

"Shake hands," Johnny quickly answered.

"What word starts with an F and ends in K that means a lot of heat and excitement?"

The principal's eyes opened really wide but before he could stop the answer, Johnny yelled, "Fire truck!"

The principal was stunned. Slowly drawing a sigh of relief, he told the teacher, "Put Johnny in the fifth grade. I got the last questions wrong."

# Message from Santa

Dear Friends,

I have been watching you very closely to see if you have been good this year, and since you have, I will be telling my elves to make some goodies for me to leave under your tree at Christmas.

I was going to bring you all those gifts from the "Twelve Days of Christmas," but we had a little problem. The nine fiddlers fiddling have come down with VD from fiddling with the eleven ladies dancing. The twelve lords a-leaping have knocked up the eight maids a-milking, and the ten pipers piping have been arrested for doing weird things to the seven swans a-swimming. And the six geese a-laying, four calling birds, three French hens, two turtledoves, and the partridge in the pear tree have me up to my sled runners in bird shit.

On top of all that, Mrs. Clause is going through menopause, eight of my reindeer are in heat, the elves have joined the gay liberation, and some people who can't read the calendar have scheduled Christmas for the fifth of January.

Maybe next year I will be able to get my shit together and bring you everything you want. This year, I suggest you get your lazy asses down to the mall before everything good is gone.

Love, Santa

# Goats

A group of Americans were traveling by tour bus through Holland. As they stopped at a cheese farm, a young guide led them through the process of cheese making, explaining that goat's milk was used. She showed the group a lovely hillside where many goats were grazing. These, she explained, were the older goats that were put out to pasture when they no longer produced.

She then asked, "What do you do in America with your older goats?"

A spry gentleman answered, "They send us on bus tours."

# The Baptist Cowgirl

A cowgirl who just moved to Texas from Arkansas walks into a bar and orders three mugs of beer. She sits in the back of the room, drinking a sip out of each one in turn. When she finishes them, she comes back to the bar and orders three more. The bartender approaches and tells the cowgirl, "You know, a mug goes flat after I draw it. It would taste better if you bought one at a time."

The cowgirl replies, "Well, you see, I have two sisters. One lives in Australia, the other in Dublin. When we left our home in Arkansas, we promised that we'd drink this way to remember the days when we drank together. So I'm drinking one beer for each of my sisters and one for myself."

The bartender admits that this is a nice custom and leaves her alone.

The cowgirl becomes a regular at the bar, and always drinks the same way. She orders three mugs of beer and drinks them in turn.

One day she comes in and orders only two mugs. All the regulars take notice and fall silent. When she comes back to the bar for a second round, the bartender says, "I don't want to intrude on your grief, but I want to offer my condolences on your loss."

The cowgirl looks quite puzzled for a moment, then the light dawns in her eyes and she laughs. "Oh, no, everyone is just fine," she explains. "It's just that my husband and I joined the Baptist church, and I had to quit drinking. It hasn't affected my sisters, though."

# Woman Volunteer

Eleven people were dangling from a rope attached to a helicopter—ten men and one woman. The rope was not strong enough to carry them all, so they decided that one had to let go because otherwise they were all going to fall.

They weren't able to choose that person until the woman gave a very touching speech. She said that she would voluntarily let go of the rope because, as a woman, she was used to giving up everything for her kids and her husband, or for men in general, and was used to making sacrifices.

As soon as she finished her speech, all the men started clapping their hands.

# Marketing

The buzzword in today's business world is MARKETING. For example, you're a woman and you see a handsome guy at a party. You go up to him and say, "I'm fantastic in bed." That is Direct Marketing.

You're at a party with a bunch of friends and see a handsome guy. One of your friends goes up to him and, pointing at you, says, "She's fantastic in bed." That is Advertising.

You see a handsome guy at a party. You go up to him and get his telephone number. The next day you call him and say, "Hi, I'm fantastic in bed." That is Telemarketing.

You see a handsome guy at a party, you straighten your dress. You walk up to him and pour him a drink. You say, "May I?" and reach up to straighten his tie, brushing your breast slightly against his arm, and then you mention, "By the way, I'm fantastic in bed." That is Public Relations.

You're at a party and you see a handsome guy. He walks up to you and says, "I hear you are fantastic in bed." That is Brand Recognition.

You're at a party and you see a handsome guy. He fancies you, but you talk him into going home with your friend. That is being a Sales Representative.

Your friend can't satisfy him, so she calls you. That is Technical Support.

You're on your way to a party when you realize that there could be a handsome guy in all the houses you are passing. So you climb onto the roof of one of the houses that is situated near the center and shout at the top of your lungs, "I'm fantastic in bed!" That is Junk Mail.

# Letters from Camp

Dear Mom and Dad,

Our scoutmaster told us to write to our parents in case you saw the flood on TV and are worried. We are okay. Only one of our tents and two sleeping bags got washed away. Luckily, none of us drowned because we were all up the mountain looking for Chad when it happened. Oh, yes—please call Chad's mother and tell her he is fine. He can't write because of the plaster cast.

I got to ride in one of the search and rescue jeeps. It was cool! We never would have found Chad in the dark if it hadn't been for the lightning. Scoutmaster Don got mad at Chad for going for a hike alone without telling anyone. Chad said he did tell him, but it was during the fire so he probably didn't hear him.

Did you know that if you put gasoline on a fire, the gasoline will blow up? The wet wood didn't burn, but one of the tents did and also some of our clothes. David is going to look weird until his hair grows back.

We will be home on Saturday if Scoutmaster Don gets the car fixed. It wasn't his fault about the wreck. The brakes worked okay when we left camp. Scoutmaster Don said that with a car that old you have to expect something to break down, which is probably why he can't get insurance on it. We think it's a neat car. He doesn't care if we get it dirty, and if it's hot sometimes he lets us ride on the fenders. It gets pretty hot with ten people in a car. He let us take turns riding in the trailer, until the highway patrol man stopped and talked to us.

Scoutmaster Don is a neat guy. Don't worry, he is a good driver. In fact, he is teaching Terry how to drive on the mountain roads where there isn't any traffic—all we ever see up there is logging trucks.

This morning all of the guys were diving off the rocks and swimming out in the lake. Scoutmaster Don wouldn't let me because I can't swim, and Chad was afraid he would sink because of his cast, so he let us take the canoe across the lake. It was great. You can still see some of the trees under the water from the flood.

And guess what? We have all passed our first merit badges. When Dave dived into the lake and cut his arm, we got to see how a tourniquet works. Wade and I threw up, but Scoutmaster Don said it probably was just food poisoning from the leftover chicken. He said he got sick that way, too, with food he ate in prison. I'm so glad he got out and became our scoutmaster. He said he figured out how to get things done better while he was doing his time.

By the way, what is a pedal-file?

I have to go now. We are going into town to mail our letters and buy some Vaseline. Don't worry about anything. We are fine, and Scoutmaster Don promised us all lots more fun.

Love, Timmy

# The Birds and the Bees

A father asked his ten-year-old son if he knew about the birds and the bees. "I don't want to know," the child said, bursting into tears. "Promise me you won't tell me about the birds and the bees."

Confused, the father asked his son what was wrong. The boy, sobbing, said, "When I was six, I got the There's No Easter Bunny speech.

"At seven, I got the There's No Tooth Fairy speech.

"When I was eight, you hit me with the There's No Santa speech.

"So, if you're going to tell me now that grownups don't really get laid, I'll have nothing to live for."

# BJ

A wife comes home early one day and catches her hubby beating off in the kitchen. She rushes over and gives him the best blow job of his life. Afterwards he asks, "We haven't had sex for over six months and now, suddenly, this. Why?"

She answers with a smug grin, "I just washed the floor this morning—I'd rather brush my teeth than clean the damn floor again."

LaVergne, TN USA
17 January 2011
212616LV00002B/1/P